Marxist Thought and the City

BOOKS BY HENRI LEFEBVRE
PUBLISHED BY THE UNIVERSITY OF MINNESOTA PRESS

Dialectical Materialism

State, Space, World: Selected Essays

Toward an Architecture of Enjoyment

The Urban Revolution

BOOKS ON HENRI LEFEBVRE
PUBLISHED BY THE UNIVERSITY OF MINNESOTA PRESS

Henri Lefebvre on Space: Architecture, Urban Research,
and the Production of Theory
ŁUKASZ STANEK

Marxist Thought and the City

Henri Lefebvre

Translated by Robert Bononno

Foreword by Stuart Elden

University of Minnesota Press
Minneapolis
London

Cet ouvrage, publié dans le cadre d'un programme d'aide à la publication, bénéficie de la participation de la Mission Culturelle et Universitaire Française aux Etats-Unis, service de l'Ambassade de France aux EU. This work received support from the publication program of the Mission Culturelle et Universitaire Française aux Etats-Unis, a department of the French Embassy in the United States.

Originally published in French as *La pensée marxiste et la ville.* Copyright 1972 by Casterman. All rights reserved.

Published by the University of Minnesota Press
111 Third Avenue South, Suite 290
Minneapolis, MN 55401-2520
http://www.upress.umn.edu

Printed in the United States of America on acid-free paper

The University of Minnesota is an equal-opportunity educator and employer.

22 21 20 19 18 17 16   10 9 8 7 6 5 4 3 2 1

Library of Congress Cataloging-in-Publication Data
Names: Lefebvre, Henri, 1901–1991, author.
Title: Marxist thought and the city / Henri Lefebvre ; translated by Robert
    Bononno ; foreword by Stuart Elden
Other titles: Pensée marxiste et la ville. English
Description: Minneapolis : University of Minnesota Press, [2016] | Includes
    bibliographical references.
Identifiers: LCCN 2016014087 | ISBN 978-0-8166-9874-5 (hc) | ISBN 978-0-8166-
    9875-2 (pb)
Subjects: LCSH: Communism and society. | Sociology, Urban. | BISAC: SOCIAL
    SCIENCE / Sociology / Urban. | SOCIAL SCIENCE / Human Geography. |
    PHILOSOPHY / Social.
Classification: LCC HX542 .L3713 2016 | DDC 307.76—dc23
LC record available at https://lccn.loc.gov/2016014087

Contents

Foreword

Stuart Elden

La pensée marxiste et la ville, here translated as *Marxist Thought and the City,* was first published in February 1972.[1] It has been largely but not entirely neglected in Anglophone debates, overshadowed by some of Lefebvre's other works and analyses by others. Its legacy elsewhere is rather different, with translations into a number of languages. Crucially, many of these were made shortly after its publication, rather than, as here, and as much of the Anglophone reception of Lefebvre has been, at several decades' distance.

In the 1960s, Lefebvre turned from his long interest in rural questions to examine the process of urbanization and urban transformation. Initially sparked by watching the dual activities of industrialization and urbanization in his home area of the Pyrenees, it soon became a major and abiding concern of his work. Although urban questions had been discussed in earlier writings, in 1968's *The Right to the City* they took center stage.[2] Closely followed by his eyewitness account of the events of May 1968, *The Explosion,* over the next six years Lefebvre produced a number of important urban-themed works: *The Urban Revolution* (1970), *Du rural à l'urbain* (1970), a second volume of *The Right to the City* titled *Espace et politique* (1972), and the present volume.[3] In 1973 *The Survival of Capitalism* appeared and—in the original French, but not in the English translation—incorporated some of the material from *The Explosion,* thus giving the text a more urban flavor in its original form.[4] In 1974 all of this work, urban and rural alike, led to its grand theoretical culmination in *The Production of Space,* before Lefebvre expanded his horizons still further with the four-volume sprawling *De l'État* (1976–78), partially translated in *State, Space, World* (2009).[5] Yet, extensive though this output is, in the same period Lefebvre published several other books, on topics including everyday life, history, difference, structuralism, Kostas Axelos, a collection on Fourier, and three short plays. A book-length manuscript from 1973 languished in a Spanish basement until its recent rediscovery and publication as *Toward an Architecture of Enjoyment* (2014).[6] The years 1968–74 are thus one of the most fertile periods in his long career, but by no means the only one. Although these works appeared in his late sixties and early seventies, he would continue to write and publish right up until his death in 1991.

The urban texts range from political manifestos to studies of processes, from detailed analyses of specific sites to theoretical development. *Marxist Thought and the City* connects in multiple ways to those other works, but it is also something of an isolated analysis. In it Lefebvre provides a detailed and synthetic reading of the work of Marx and Engels concerning "the city and urban problems." Yet, as Lefebvre immediately concedes, these discussions are "never systematized," they are "fragments," "scattered passages" in the midst of wider analyses. Nonetheless, he suggests that there is enough there to justify this project, with the central theme being "the city, and consequently, the urban problematic within the theoretical framework of historical materialism." It is an unusual work in his corpus, being devoted to a close reading and exegesis of work by others. It is better integrated and, arguably, better written than many of his other works. But it is not just a study of what Marx and Engels had to say about the city: using the city as a lens, it provides an overall view of key aspects of the critique of political economy.

Lefebvre had, early in his career, collaborated with Norbert Guterman on thematically organized selections from the writings

of Marx and Hegel. Guterman was a Jewish émigré from Eastern
Europe, and a multilinguist. They also translated and presented
Lenin's notebooks on Hegel's dialectic, as well as writing texts together. Unfortunately, their work was cut short by Guterman's
enforced move to the United States shortly before World War II
broke out. They kept up a correspondence until Guterman's death.
Yet their 1934 *Morceaux choisis de Karl Marx* did not contain a
section on urban or spatial questions, nor did the much later
Karl Marx, Œuvres choisies in two volumes in 1963 and 1966. So,
in 1972 Lefebvre makes good on this omission. Indeed, one way
to understand Lefebvre's work in general terms is as a series of
contributions that develop Marxist thought in different and frequently neglected directions: everyday life, the rural, the urban,
space, the state, the worldwide. But he immediately qualifies his
aim here: this book is not merely a selection of relevant passages,
but a "thematic reading." And the reading is for a purpose in the
present and for the future, rather than an antiquarian assemblage:

> I have examined these texts on behalf of the present and the pos-
> sible; and that is, precisely, Marx's method, the one he recom-
> mended so that the past (events and documents) might live on
> and serve the future.

This present purpose is important: Ninety years after the death
of Marx, Lefebvre is well aware that the analyses need resituating
to speak to the contemporary condition. Forty years on from this
work, and twenty-five years after Lefebvre's death, further developments would render that need even more pressing, though it is
striking how much of what energized Lefebvre remains an issue
today.

The book comprises five chapters. In the first, Lefebvre provides a reading of Engels's *The Condition of the Working Class in
England*. In the second, he outlines the specifically urban aspects
of the division of labor. The third chapter discusses the wider
project of a "critique of political economy" in relation to urban
themes. This translation then has an additional chapter to the

original edition, "Engels and Utopia," which was intended for the book but was removed because of the length of the manuscript and included in *Espace et politique* instead.[7] It was restored to later editions of the text, and is included here. In it Lefebvre discusses Engels's *The Housing Question,* among other texts. The final chapter is a wide-ranging study of the question of land ownership, drawing together themes from Lefebvre's long-standing interest in rural questions with the focus on the urban.

The reading, as this brief outline indicates, ranges across Marx and Engels's work. The discussions extend from the "1844 manuscripts" to early works taking a distance from their contemporaries, through historical analyses, to the *Grundrisse, Capital,* and the *Theories of Surplus Value,* and many of Engels's separate works, including the *Anti-Dühring.* The texts, he suggests, only reveal their insights by being considered within Marx and Engels's thought as a whole. Lefebvre is especially good at situating the analysis of *Capital* in the wider framework envisaged in the *Grundrisse.* But he is not trying to suggest that Marx is an urban sociologist or geographer, and generally he insists on reading him as a whole, with a resistance to any specialized reading of Marx as economist, philosopher, historian, and so on. Lefebvre also offers some illuminating comments on the Marx–Engels relation, stressing the themes that Engels developed independently of Marx, and the initial contributions he made to their collaborative work. Themes treated also include the history of variant city forms, from the "Asiatic" to the cities of antiquity, the Middle Ages, and the modern period; the complicated town–country relationship; and the *critique* of political economy. The emphasis in the last is Lefebvre's own, following the lead of Marx, and in this volume we have, perhaps more than in any other translated work of his, a sustained reading of political economy and Marxism generally.

The book links to many of Lefebvre's other studies. We have, for example, an emphasis on the reciprocal relation between capital and ground rent, and a stress on land as the "material support of societies," an analysis that is materialist but not reductively economic. These trade on his detailed work, mainly in the 1950s, on ground rent and rural sociology, largely but not entirely neglected in English translation.[8] There are discussions of surplus value in the rural and urban context, in terms of production, appropriation, and distribution, a theme also found in *The Urban Revolution* and *De l'État*. There is also a strong emphasis on the move from the rural to the urban. He stresses Marx's claim in the *Grundrisse* that in the modern period what we are experiencing "is the urbanization of the countryside, not ruralization of the city as in antiquity."[9] For Lefebvre, "this is a decisive formula that illustrates the essential dialectical movement" of the transformation. Lefebvre's *The Urban Revolution,* despite its title, is more about a revolution *of* the urban than a revolution *in* the urban, and had developed these themes in some detail. As he stresses here, trading on the opening lines of that book, in the present moment we are experiencing "the complete urbanization of society . . . a revolutionary process because it transforms both the surface of the globe and society." The introduction of the globe is important. Lefebvre generally stressed the extension of phenomena to what he called the worldwide, *le mondial,* seeing that as a scale. When he uses the word *le global* he usually means the total or the general, a level of analysis. Too quickly appropriating Lefebvre as anticipating globalization misses this dual distinction: the world versus the global, the scale versus the level. Nonetheless, what Lefebvre talks about with the world, and he and his colleagues called *mondialisation,* that is, the process of becoming worldwide, certainly provides important insights into the process we now call globalization. These questions are more fully explored in his later work, but there are important anticipations here. Right toward the end of the text, for example, he begins to connect the concerns examined here to the work to come on the production of space. As he stresses, capitalism and its survival are dependent on the reproduction of the relations of production, and the role of the production of space in this process. "Generalized urbanization is an aspect of this colossal expansion." We can then trace a line from this book on the urban to *The Survival of Capitalism, The Production of Space,* and the English collection *State, Space, World* through to some of Lefebvre's last works.

In the forty-plus years since Lefebvre's book appeared, a wide range of analyses of the urban and other spatial questions have been developed. Lefebvre's book was published the same year as Manuel Castells's *La question urbaine,* and the year before David Harvey's *Social Justice and the City,* two texts that did much to generate a Marxist geography.[10] Too many works have been produced within and beyond this tradition to even attempt a survey here. Nobody would today write a book titled "Marxist Thought and the City" without an analysis of many of those figures. But many of them have made use of Lefebvre's work, especially his analyses of the right to the city, the urban revolution, and the production of space. In Anglophone literatures at least, much of that has followed the translation of those works (entirely out of sequence) in 1996, 2003, and 1991. Nobody could write a book titled "Marxist Thought and the City" today without a discussion of Lefebvre's pioneering work.[11]

Yet the analyses here are not merely of historical or theoretical interest. If you were to ask urban social scientists today about the pressing issues in their work, you would expect that, among others, they would suggest the interrelation of urbanization and industrialization; the extension of the urban beyond central agglomerations, and the implications this has for thinking about the urban/rural divide; the question of scarcity in the housing market and the politics of rent, including pricing the working poor out of the places they work; and resources and environmental degradation. Anyone interested in those topics will find much to value in this book.[12] Such issues, though, are crucially situated within a wider analysis. As Lefebvre notes, following Engels, the housing shortage is a result of wider questions in the opposition between town and country resulting from the capitalist mode of production. Yet, as he also notes in relation to the use of Marx's thought in understanding the production of space at the world scale, its relevance endures because it is useful, because it helps us to understand contradictions and conflicts. Otherwise we should simply abandon it. In his situation of specific urban questions in a wider context, showing connections and tensions, and providing a framework for their analysis, Lefebvre's work remains of enduring importance. *Marxist Thought and the City,* now more widely available in Robert Bononno's fine translation, is a central piece of that contribution.

Introductory Note

Henri Lefebvre

Throughout the work of Marx and Engels there are references to the city and urban problems, but these references were never systematized by the founders of scientific socialism. They do not form a body of doctrine that would rest on a given methodology or a specialized "discipline" such as philosophy, political economy, ecology, or sociology. Generally speaking, these fragments are presented in terms of other, broader topics: the division of labor, productive forces and the relations of production, historical materialism. This project began by rereading the work of Marx and Engels in its entirety to assemble these scattered passages. There is nothing inherently special about this "rereading." It can't be said to be "literal" because it is intended to assemble fragments, while exposing the concepts and categories of theoretical thought shared by those texts. Nor can it be said to be "symptomatic," because there is no question of identifying, in the thought of Marx and Engels, a latent content, something left unsaid that it is up to the reader to discover. Rather, my reading, or rereading, has been thematic. The theme under consideration is the city and, consequently, the urban problematic within the theoretical framework of historical materialism.

Such an assemblage of texts would have little interest in itself; it would merely sustain official dogmatism and the reigning form of scholasticism if it didn't stimulate further investigation and guide our response. Do these references, these concepts, address the current problems of urban reality in all their magnitude? Has there been anything new in this field during the past century? Clearly, a thematic reading is what is called for; it will possess a significance and scope that "selected passages" could never provide.

Marxist Thought and the City

The Situation of the Working Class in England

The year is 1845. The elements and signs of a new reality—industrialization, the working class, capitalism—are multiplying. For several years now Friedrich Engels (he was twenty-four in 1845) had been interested in economic and social issues, which he considered more important than the philosophical questions with which he had begun his studies. With Karl Marx he had only one, short meeting over the course of a few days in 1844, in Paris. At the time, Engels was not yet working with Marx on the construction of "Marxism." In fact, he preempted his friend-to-be on the path they would take together, one that began in 1845.

The book, *The Condition of the Working Class in England*, had been in preparation for a long time.[1] In 1842, Engels had published a series of important articles about England and its transformation into an industrial power and the dramatic (negative) aspects of that development.[2] In them he identified England's originality compared to the situation in France and Germany at the time. In England the characteristic features of a new society were taking shape and beginning to cohere, and the predominance of economic factors was the first and most important of them. In France and Germany, a theoretical and political revolution was under way, a double revolution that could not be separated from the "industrial revolution" in England; it "expressed" this in thought and action but was distinct in the sense that the unfolding of historical circumstances had separated theory from practice, and political practice from social (economic) practice.

Engels's introduction begins quite remarkably with an idea

that he would develop and clarify in the course of the book: "The history of the proletariat in England begins with the second half of the last century, with the invention of the steam engine and of machinery for working cotton. These inventions gave rise, as is well known, to an industrial revolution."[3] This expression, which would later become so well known, is used here for the first time by Engels in 1845. He adds that he is not concerned with the history of this revolution, its importance in the world, or its future. In this work he is limiting himself, provisionally and temporarily, to the situation of the English proletariat. The introduction of the use of industrial machinery transformed the existence of weavers, ruining many families who worked honestly and diligently in the countryside, near the cities but somewhat isolated. These energetic and sturdy individuals were rarely able to read, much less write, but went to church regularly and "never talked politics, never conspired, never thought, delighted in physical exercises, listened with inherited reverence when the Bible was read" (17). They appeared to be very human and were, in a sense. And yet, weren't they already simple machines in the service of the aristocracy? The industrial revolution had completely reduced the workers to the role of machines, "taking from them the last trace of independent activity" (ibid.), but formally notifying them that they should "demand a position worthy of men" (ibid.). In France, politics, in England, industry had dragged the classes, plunged into apathy, through the whirlwind of history.

The causes of the revolutionary transformation were new technologies (primarily the "spinning jenny" and "spinning mule" in the late eighteenth century, their subsequent development, and of course the steam engine). This gave rise to the great industrial and commercial cities of the British Empire (36). Engels assumed that *technological* causes were the origin of this upheaval.

In *The Condition of the Working Class in England*, Engels describes, analyzes, and exposes for the first time the nature of capitalism in a large country. The importance he assigns to urban phenomena is surprising, however. Apart from those chapters explicitly devoted to such phenomena (among others, the very long second chapter), they appear from the beginning of the book. Engels demonstrates the existence of a twofold centralizing tendency in capitalism. The concentration of population accompanies that of capital (chapter 1, "The Industrial Proletariat," 33–34). Villages are formed around an average-size factory; this results in population growth and, inevitably, other industrialists will arrive to make use of (to exploit) this labor power. The village becomes a small town and the small town grows larger. "The greater the town, the greater its advantages" (34). All the elements of industry are gathered together here: the workers, the channels of communication (canals, railroads, highways), the transport of raw materials, machinery and technology, markets, the stock exchange. This results in the astonishingly rapid rise of the large industrial cities. Although salaries remain lower in rural areas and there is competition between the city and the countryside, the advantage goes to the city. This centralizing tendency is by far the stronger factor and every industry created in a rural area bears within it the seeds of an industrial city. Virtually every industrial region of England is but a single city; it will become so in reality if this "mad rush" lasts for another century. "Since commerce and manufacture attain their most complete development in these great towns, their influence upon the proletariat is also most clearly observable here. Here the centralization of property has reached the highest point; here the morals and customs of the good old times are most completely obliterated" (ibid.).

Let's stop a moment to examine these early texts and their context. The year is 1845, a year of intense theoretical ferment. In February of that year there appeared, in Frankfurt, *The Holy Family*, in which Marx and Engels refuted the proponents of abstraction and historical idealism, the philosophers for whom the human masses are passive observers of the process of "man's" creation of his social being. In January 1845 Marx, who had been thrown out of Paris, settled in Brussels. In April, Engels joined him there and over the summer they traveled together to England. Engels

showed Marx what he had described and analyzed in his book,
which had been published in Leipzig. Toward the end of the year,
they started work on *The German Ideology,* which would com-
bine earlier research, condense their criticism of various "ideologies" (philosophy, political economy, idealized history), and offer
a new approach to the human being, considered as someone who
produced himself through his labor—historical materialism. As
described in a subsequent chapter, the questions concerning the
city appeared with considerable force in the formulation of historical materialism. In the very beginning of *The German Ideology,* immediately after the well-known lines (still philosophical
although they extend beyond and reject classical philosophy)—
"Men can be distinguished from animals by consciousness, by religion or anything else you like. They themselves begin to distinguish themselves from animals as soon as they begin to *produce*
their means of subsistence . . ."—there begins the discussion of the
city.[4] These considerations are mostly retrospective, which corresponds to the method Marx would later make explicit: clarifica-
tion of the past on the basis of current events. From here on, his
discussion is focused primarily on the relationship between the
city and the country in antiquity and the Middle Ages. We will
see how emphasizing the relationship of conflict in his consideration of the past was an essential component of his argument and
an achievement of historical materialism. But in Marx, questions
about the modern city never attain the scope they do in Engels's
first work. There are several entry points in Marxist thought. So
why is there no more than a single line of thought, a necessary but
always identical approach, traced by some authority, and which
must be followed slavishly? To claim that Engels contributed to
the formation of so-called Marxist thought, to defend his memory by showing that he did not merely play second fiddle but was
an original thinker (and even situated prominently at the dawn of
"Marxist thought"), is not to impoverish that line of thought. On
the contrary, it would imply a struggle against such dogmatic and
scholastic impoverishment.

In the section "The Great Towns," Engels discovers urban reality in all its horror. Yet, this reality is never identified with ordinary disorder, much less with evil or "social" sickness, as found in many literary and scientific texts up to the present day. Engels treats London, Manchester, and other English cities as the effect of causes and reasons that can be discovered and, therefore, controlled (through understanding initially and then through revolutionary action). The bourgeoisie holds capital, which is to say, the means of production. It makes use of them, determines the conditions of their productive use. Without any deprecatory prejudices, Engels reveals the powerful contrasts within urban reality, the juxtaposition of wealth and poverty, the splendor and ugliness (ugliness and poverty are given an intense, pathos-filled coloration because of their proximity). He begins enthusiastically, "I know nothing more imposing than the view which the Thames offers during the ascent from the sea to London Bridge. . . . all this is so vast, so impressive, that a man cannot collect himself, but is lost in the marvel of England's greatness before he sets foot upon English soil" (36). Centralization increased the power of those thousands of workers a hundredfold; it multiplied the effectiveness of their capabilities. But this prodigious social wealth, which came to fruition under the economic and political control of the English bourgeoisie, was accompanied by sacrifice. Londoners "have been forced to sacrifice the best qualities of their human nature to bring to pass all the marvels of civilization which crowd their city" (ibid.). The powers that slumbered within them have been suppressed so that "a few might be developed more fully and multiply through union with those of others. The very turmoil of the streets has something repulsive" (ibid.). Aren't these people, from all walks of life and all classes of society, *all* human beings, possessing the same abilities, the same interest in happiness? "And have they not, in the end, to seek happiness in the same way, by the same means? And still they crowd by one another as though they had nothing in common" (37). Never had such brutal indifference, such unfeeling isolation, such blinkered egotism, displayed itself with such impudence. Here, atomization is pushed to the extreme.

Thus, Engels immediately introduces the theme of the "solitary crowd" and atomization, the problematic of the street. The concept of alienation was never abstract for him (separated); he saw it as something concrete.

In these texts by Engels, whose directness detracts from their scientific nature only for those who fetishize scientificity, those who cannot tolerate any aspect of "lived experience" as part of their understanding, alienation itself is not named. The philosophical concept is not present. That he was familiar with it is made clear by his philosophical studies. But it is something he presents in its actuality, he sees it as an element of social practice.

Did he associate it with labor? Implicitly, yes; explicitly, no. It was as if Engels the economist, from the start of his career, knew that productive labor, no matter how necessary, was in itself insufficient. It gives rise to a society. The relations of production, of course, mark that society with their imprint, their domination, the power of a dominating class. The society they engender is not external. London is commerce, the global market, generalized traffic together with its consequences. It is the force that overwhelms the weak and the wealth that creates poverty; but it is also civilization and its miracles. Engels never believed the baby should be thrown out with the bathwater.

His freedom of thought is all the greater when he describes, in their smallest and yet revealing details, the result of this prodigious accumulation of power and wealth for the workers—the great modern city. But it is not the working class alone that is affected as a class, it is society as a whole, including its rulers, those who make use of the wealth produced because they control the means of production and the labor force. A form of whiplash occurs. "The social war, the war of each against all, is here openly declared" (ibid.). People consider one another solely in terms of their usefulness; everyone exploits everyone else. The strongest, the capitalists, appropriate *everything* (ibid.). In this generalized

warfare, capital, direct or indirect ownership of the means of subsistence and production, is the weapon of struggle. Those who
have no capital, no money, are irrelevant. If a man cannot find
work, he can steal or starve to death, "in which case the police will
take care that he does so in a quiet and inoffensive manner" (38).
In this way, the urban space and its contrasts, its liberties and fa-
talities, is a repressive space: the space of "social crime," which the
English worker believed the whole of society committed perpet-
ually (ibid.).

Having described the poverty of London's poor neighbor-
hoods, the poverty that his friend Marx would share a few years
later, Engels goes on to describe the other cities of the three king-
doms. Dublin, "a city, the approach to which from the sea is as
charming as that of London is imposing" (45). The city has many
beautiful features, Engels writes, but the poor sections are among
the most repugnant. Perhaps the national character of the Irish
plays a role but there is nothing specific about poverty in Dublin; it resembles that of all the world's large cities. Likewise with
Edinburgh, "whose superb situation, which has won it the title of
the Modern Athens, and whose brilliant aristocratic quarter
in the New Town, contrast strongly with the foul wretchedness
of the poor in the Old Town" (46). Liverpool, "with all its commerce, wealth, and grandeur yet treats its workers with the same
barbarity" (48). He provides similar descriptions of Sheffield, Bir-
mingham, and Glasgow.

On Manchester and its particular situation, Engels spends considerably more time, for both theoretical and personal reasons. It
was here that British industry began and Manchester remained its
center; the Manchester stock exchange was the economic barom-
eter for the country. Modern technologies were perfected by the
cotton industry in Lancashire: the use of natural forces, the elimination of manual labor by machinery, the division of labor. "If we
recognize in these three elements that which is characteristic of
modern manufacture, we must confess that the cotton industry
has remained in advance of all other branches of industry from

the beginning down to the present day" (54). It was here that the consequences of industrialization were felt most deeply and the industrial proletariat most fully realized. "Hence because Manchester is the classic type of a modern manufacturing town, and because I know it as intimately as my own native town, more intimately than most of its residents know it, we shall make a longer stay here" (ibid.).

The old urban center grew considerably. The number of surrounding towns grew, and these were even more industrialized than the city center. The management of business dealings was left to Manchester, while the towns were populated by workers and "petty tradesmen." There was formed an enormous agglomeration of workers' quarters holding up to a hundred thousand inhabitants. Between them ran factories, but also gardens and villas, most often in the Elizabethan style, "which is to the Gothic precisely what the Anglican Church is to the Apostolic Roman Catholic" (56). The capitalist order engenders urban chaos.

It is important to note that Engels does not analyze the situation of the historical cities on the Continent—Italy, Flanders, France, Germany. Those cities predate industrial capitalism as political cities (administrative and military) or are associated with commercial capital; they were subjected to the assault of industrial and capitalist forces that arose externally and often in opposition to them. Manchester is quite different, in the more general context of England, because of its privileged position (in the nineteenth century) on the world market. Trade and industry grew simultaneously in and around the city. The characteristic features that Engels finds there have general application, however: segregation and the breakdown of the city center.

Spontaneous, possibly "unconscious," segregation is no less severe. It marks both the concrete city and its image: "The town itself is peculiarly built, so that a person may live in it for years, and go in and out daily without coming into contact with a working-people's quarter or even with workers" (57). The bourgeoisie of this imperially democratic England has succeeded in creating this masterpiece: concealing the sight of a poverty it would find offensive. It dissimulates the repressive exploitation and the result of that exploitation. "By unconscious tacit agreement, as well as with outspoken conscious determination, the working-people's quarters are sharply separated from the sections of the city reserved for the middle class" (ibid.). At the same time, Manchester's center harbors a large commercial quarter, which is "lonely and deserted during the night, only watchmen and policemen traverse its narrow lanes with their dark lanterns" (58).

Need it be said that today, in the second half of the twentieth century, decades of urban studies (economic, sociological, historical, anthropological) have largely confirmed Engels's view? (We could say his "vision" if it weren't customary to contrast the term to that of scientific "theory.") Needless to say, much has changed. The British Empire has collapsed. The global market, immensely greater in size, has seen the entrance of other actors, whose industries are more or less associated with democracy. This globalizing process (industrialization and urbanization) is no less generalized, and Engels was able to identify and conceptualize its development based on a kind of sample or typical reality: Manchester—segregation and decomposition.

He brilliantly demonstrates how that strange mixture of order and chaos explains the urban space and how that space exposes the essence of society. He provides a detailed description, street by street, quarter by quarter, starting with the stock exchange. "In this way one who knows Manchester can infer the adjoining districts, from the appearance of the thoroughfare, but one is seldom in a position to catch from the street a glimpse of the real laboring districts" (59). In short, prior to the industrial era, society hid its shameful parts, its faults and its vices: madness, prostitution, disease. It hid them in the depths of the metropolis. Bourgeois society, however, concealed its means of subsistence, its active and productive part. This hypocritical attitude is more or less common to all the great cities, "but at the same time I have never seen so systematic a shutting out of the working

class from the thoroughfares, so tender a concealment of everything which might affront the eye and the nerves of the bourgeoisie, as in Manchester" (ibid.). Was this deliberate? The construction of Manchester does not follow any precise plan. "And yet, in
other respects, Manchester is less built according to a plan, after
official regulations, is more an outgrowth of accident, than any
other city" (ibid.). Yet, when Engels considers the middle class,
which hurries to claim that its workers are better off than those
found elsewhere in the world, he wonders if the "liberal manufacturers" are completely unaware of such innocent "methods of
construction."

According to Engels, a specific order, that of industrial production managed by the bourgeoisie (within the context of the
relations of capitalist production, Marx would explicitly state),
engenders a specific disorder, urban disorder. Can there come a
moment when this order ceases to dominate the chaos it brings
about, when disorder overwhelms order? Engels suspects as
much; he suggests it when he closely examines a map of Manchester and its surroundings. Here, he introduces the concept of
urbanism. "Of the irregular cramming together of dwellings in
ways which defy all rational plan, of the tangle in which they are
crowded literally one upon the other, it is impossible to convey an
idea" (60). The confusion reaches its apogee; wherever the urbanism of an earlier era had left some free space, now "every scrap
of space left by the old way of building has been filled up and
patched over until not a foot of land is left to be further occupied"
(ibid.). This congestion gives rise to pollution of the air, water, and
all the surrounding space.

"Everything which here arouses horror and indignation is of
recent origin, belongs to the industrial epoch" (65). Old Manchester has been abandoned by its former inhabitants; industry has
crammed those old houses with hordes of workers; it has built
on every parcel of land available to shelter the masses it draws
from the countryside and from Ireland. "The industrial epoch
alone enables the owners of these cattle sheds to rent them for

high prices to human beings" (66). The worker freed from serf-dom was treated as an object by industry. It enclosed him within walls falling into ruin, for which he was forced to pay a high price. Every inch of space was used. "The value of land rose with the blossoming out of manufacture, and the more it rose, the more madly was the work of building up carried on" (ibid.). Having an-alyzed the old town, Engels goes on to examine its more recent outgrowths. "Here all the features of a city are lost" (ibid.). Single rows of houses, like islands, join together and we enter an inter-minable array of alleyways, dead ends, back lanes, and courtyards. Whereas in the old town accident presided over the grouping of houses and each house was built without any concern for its neighbors, occasionally a kind of order seems to emerge. Around an urban center? Not, says Engels, around the courtyards, which are surrounded by streets, covered passages, and entranceways. Certain liberals see in these courtyards a masterpiece of urban architecture, claiming that they provide air and light by creating a large number of small public parks (68n). In fact, they have be-come sewers, containers for waste and filth, for the regulations that apply to the thoroughfares do not apply here. When contrac-tors build housing for workers around interior alleys and court-yards, only a small number of the cottages have access to adequate ventilation (68–69, where a map of a typical street is presented). The best-paid workers are exploited by renting the cottages that are best situated at higher rents. The builders and owners, more-over, make few, if any, repairs. They don't want to reduce their in-come. Because of the instability of the labor supply (crises), whole streets often remain empty. Parsimony governs their construction. Houses remain unoccupied. Renters change lodgings frequently and the houses last no more than forty years, for that is how they are designed. During their final years, they reach a last stage of "inhabitableness" (71). This corresponds to an enormous waste of invested capital and the destruction of men and resources.

Engels discovers urban order and disorder (of the city and housing) and finds them *significant*. They are revelatory of society as a whole. "The manner in which the need of a shelter is satisfied furnishes a standard for the manner in which all other necessities are supplied" (78). This need, therefore, is something more than the others: it is a privileged witness. If we closely examine the food and clothing of the workers, we find the same features; what is true of housing is true of food and clothing. "In the great towns of England everything may be had of the best, but it costs money; and the workman, who must keep house on a couple of pence, cannot afford much expense" (80). Certain details aggravate the situation of the workers, details that are minor in appearance. Paid Saturday evening, they arrive at the markets when the middle-class shoppers have already selected the best and the least expensive produce. By a series of refined mechanisms, direct exploitation is doubled by a form of indirect exploitation and extends from the enterprise (the workshop, the factory) to every feature of daily life in the urban context.

At the end of this long chapter, Engels summarizes his thought; rather, he claims to have summarized it, whereas it goes off in a direction that is as surprising as it is illuminating. The great towns, he writes, are inhabited primarily by workers (today this proposition would raise several objections), who own nothing. They live from day to day on their salary. Society, such as it is, leaves them to satisfy their needs and those of their family; it does not supply them with the means to do so efficiently and permanently (85). This results in the instability of the condition of the worker; the working class of the great cities "offers a graduated scale of conditions in life" (ibid.), a life that is momentarily bearable in spite of the hard work and limitless poverty, which can result in starvation. The average, Engels states, is much nearer the worst than it is to the best. Yet, these are not fixed categories. The situation of the workers is such that any worker can experience every step along the entire scale, from relative comfort to extreme poverty. In general, the homes of the workers are poorly arranged, poorly constructed, poorly maintained, badly ventilated, humid, and unhealthy. "The inhabitants are confined to the smallest possible space" (ibid.). In most cases, an entire family sleeps in one room. Interior furnishing is poverty-stricken and we fall by degrees until we reach the complete absence of necessary furniture.

Among the reasons for this situation, Engels identifies *competition* among the workers (individuals, ages, and groups, because the Irish form a mass who will accept the worst conditions) and the economic and social *structure* of *capitalism*. Capitalism requires a reserve of unemployed workers, except during periods of prosperity and economic growth. This "unemployment cushion" (as it is commonly referred to today by economists) is doubly necessary: to put continuous pressure on wages and to respond to seasonal fluctuations in demand and the market. During times of crisis, this mass becomes enormous and even the best workers can go without work. Consequently, industrial cities contain a "reserve army" of workers (96). This misery, which is both temporary (for individuals) and perpetual (for the class), contributes to the "picturesque" disorder and animation of the poor quarters of the industrial cities. The surplus population resorts to a wide range of activities: odd jobs, portage, as well as begging and theft. Begging assumes a particular character. The people wander the streets, singing a lament or asking for charity with a short speech. The mendicants of the workers' quarters live solely from the generosity of other workers. Sometimes an "entire family takes up position in a busy street, and without uttering a word, lets the mere sight of its helplessness plead for it" (98). But it is on Saturday evening that the workers' quarters reveal their "mysteries" and the other classes stay away. If one of these "excess men" has courage enough and passion to engage in open conflict with society and "to reply with declared war upon the bourgeoisie to the disguised war which the bourgeoisie wages upon him" (ibid.), then what does he do? He robs, plunders, murders. Competition, the expression of the war of all against all, runs rampant in modern bourgeois society; it is a war for life, for existence, for *everything* (87), and entails a life-and-death struggle, which sets the classes and the individual members of those classes against one another.

Here, the modern reader, 125 years later, may express surprise. In these pages, Engels describes, spontaneously, the modern city at its birth, pictured as he experienced it. One hundred and twenty-five years later, has this "ambiance," this "climate" changed at all? One need only have resided a short while in an American city to answer the question, even if, in our European cities, the strategy of the ruling classes has transported the workers to the surrounding areas, where they stagnate, isolated, in a repressive peace. In Europe, who can ignore them? The workers (manual or white-collar) are parked liked automobiles. In the colossal cities of North America, the dramatic picture left us by Engels is truer than ever before. Violence reigns, each bars the path of the other; the black proletariat and the Puerto Rican community continue to experience complete deprivation, but the members of those groups and classes compete among themselves, just as the bourgeoisie competes with itself.

The great industrial city, for Engels, is effectively a source of immorality and a school of crime, but the moralists who lash out against it deflect attention from the true causes of this situation. "If they should admit that poverty, insecurity, overwork, forced work, are the chief ruinous influences, they would have to draw the conclusion, then let us give the poor property, guarantee their subsistence, make laws against overwork, and this the bourgeoisie dare not formulate" (131). It is much easier to incriminate the city, or general immorality, or the forces of evil, than to focus the attack where it belongs: politics. Engels rejected moralism and preaching. For Engels, it was natural and inevitable that the situation created by a class, the bourgeoisie (possibly "unconsciously," but that was merely a detail once it began to benefit from the situation), would bring about alcoholism, prostitution, and crime. It is in this way that contempt for the social order came about, being most evident in the extreme case of crime. "If the influences demoralizing to the working-man act more powerfully, more concentratedly than usual, he becomes an offender" (140). Where is there room for the "family life" recommended by moralists? The worker cannot escape the family; he must live as a family. He is not the one who can dissolve family life, but he experiences it as negligence and contempt. This is evident from reading the newspaper; the news is significant (142). Is this bad? Is this good? These are derisive questions. In a country such as this, social war has broken out. Each sees the other as an enemy. "The enemies are dividing gradually into two great camps—the bourgeoisie on the one hand, the workers on the other" (143). In the urban context, the class struggle, for Engels, cannot be separated from generalized violence, from a war in which everyone is your enemy. This war, he adds, should not surprise us for it is merely the application of the principle of competition. "But it may very well surprise us that the bourgeoisie remains so quiet and composed in the face of the rapidly gathering storm-clouds, that it can read all these things daily in the papers without, we will not say indignation at such a social condition, but fear of its consequences, of a universal outburst of that which manifests itself symptomatically from day to day in the form of crime" (ibid.). Class prejudice blinds an entire class of mankind: the bourgeoisie. One fine day, the property-holding class is going to be surprised: "Meanwhile, the development of the nation goes its way whether the bourgeoisie has eyes for it or not, and will surprise the property-holding class one day with things not dreamed of in its philosophy" (ibid.). And this in spite of the fact that, in the picture given us by Engels, the police play a significant role. Criminality in the cities justifies its presence. In truth, it keeps watch over the social order, of which disorder is a component. But one day, for Engels, disorder will sweep away the order of which it is the expression to create a new order. This will be the big surprise.

One hundred and twenty-five years later we know that the bourgeoisie had its surprise, several times in fact and, initially, in 1871. We know that these surprises escaped the world of dreams and led to its political education. We know that the political education of the classes is a long-term process and that the ruling class, which also possesses "culture," science, and ideology, may retain its lead for many years. What is so surprising today is that Engels, with all the freshness of revolutionary thought and sensibility, expressing "lived experience" without having passed through the harsh school of theoretical concepts and political setbacks, spontaneously situates himself beyond good and evil. Some readers detect a kind of morality in his writing, but they are reading into it their own; the traces of moralism vanish from page to page. His way of evoking the criminal worker brings to mind Stendhal writing about the Italian Renaissance or Nietzsche extolling the expenditure of energy over stagnation. Moralism—that of the bourgeoisie and that of the labor bureaucracy—has not yet reached that point. Years later, this lively expression becomes muted; revolutionary thought becomes prudent, tactically precautionary. It dissipates. And this phenomenon is exacerbated by the fact that its center shifts, becomes located in the places of work and production. But this process has not yet been completed, is not even anticipated or foreseeable, in 1845. Rather, it is the effect of the subsequent *reduction* of revolutionary and Marxist thought that takes place during the twentieth century.

Its strongest expression, in Engels, occurs in 1845, when Marx has yet to contrast Hegel with Feuerbach (this is not without importance but is, nonetheless, distant from social and political practice). "The workers begin to feel as a class, as a whole; they begin to perceive that, though feeble as individuals, they form a power united; their separation from the bourgeoisie, the development of views peculiar to the workers and corresponding to their position in life, is fostered, the consciousness of oppression awakens, and the workers attain social and political importance. The great cities are the birthplaces of labor movements; in them the workers first began to reflect upon their own condition, and to struggle against it; in them the opposition between proletariat and bourgeoisie first made itself manifest" (133).

2

The City and the Division of Labor

It would be worthwhile to closely compare the writings of Marx and Engels on the same topic, within the same problematic. Take the "Critique of Political Economy," for example. It is generally acknowledged that Engels's article, which appeared in 1844 with the title "Outline for a Critique of Political Economy," initiated the line of thought commonly referred to as "Marxism."

The notable differences might reveal something found in these texts but left unsaid. Almost all the commentators have emphasized their commonality rather than their differences. By "difference" I don't mean divergence or disagreement, much less conflict. Overall, interpretations have tended to favor uniformity. The thought of the founders has been filtered, skimmed, pasteurized. The tiniest germ of spontaneity has been eliminated, the good with the bad. The work moved forward similar to the way in which the dairy industry approached unpasteurized milk, retaining only what is sterile, hygienic, carefully homogenized, easily digestible but lacking in flavor and bite.

Engels confronts theory with reality, economic thought with economic practice. He places "lived experience" (in trade, in industry, and in proletarian existence in a context where capital is predominant) and the expression of that same reality in political economy side by side. And he criticizes "lived experience" without thought and thought without life, which is to say, without practice.

Marx, on the other hand, contrasts the major theoretical positions at the highest level of abstraction: those of Hegel and Feuerbach, as well as Smith and Ricardo, their concepts and ideas.

When Marx began working with Engels, the speculative naïveté disappeared, to be replaced by humor and a touch of immoralism. In *The Holy Family* (1844), for example, written after Marx and Engels first met (although Engels contributed little to the volume), the tone becomes light, ironic. If the well-known fragment on the relation between real fruit and the speculative idea of fruit corresponds to the theoretical scope Marx had already achieved, other pages reflect the very concrete information Engels had acquired about the way life and society were really lived. For example, the well-known polemic directed against philosophical idealism, which targets Szeliga and his interpretation of Eugène Sue's *The Mysteries of Paris*. If Mr. Szeliga were familiar with the archives of the Parisian police, if he had read the *Mémoires* of Vidocq, he would have known that the police did not only use servants, that they were not used solely for the most rudimentary tasks, that "it does not stop at the door or where the masters are in negligé, but creeps under their sheets next to their naked body in the shape of a femme galante or even of a legitimate wife. In Sue's novel the police spy 'Bras rouge' plays a leading part in the story".[1] There is no naïveté in these remarks, which highlight the naïveté of the speculative and critical philosophers.

Nonetheless, in this critique of critique, even when it concerns *The Mysteries of Paris*, the city as such is absent, or nearly so. It is a question of a process: for or against "mankind," for or against "consciousness" and the idea of history, for or against spiritualism and materialism, for or against dogmatism and the old Germanic-Christian spirit, for or against the state as conceived by Hegel, and so on.

In the *Economic and Philosophic Manuscripts of 1844*, Marx clumsily but forcefully develops the theoretical confrontation between:

(a) metaphysics (ontology) and anthropology, knowledge of organic and natural being

   (b) philosophy (philosophy of history and history of philosophy)
      and political economy, the science of social practice and
      contemporary society

   (c) French political criticism (revolutionary, Jacobin) and the
      scientific research on wealth begun in England and, finally,
      the conceptual power of German thought (which Marx
      himself continued but whose heritage he believed would be
      used by the working class)

   (d) the Hegelian theory of "man," who produces himself over
      the course of history, through work and struggle, and
      Feuerbach's theory of "man," a natural being, sensitive and
      sentient, a being of needs and pleasures

In the *Economic and Philosophic Manuscripts of 1844,* this generalized confrontation unfolded on a "pure" intellectual level. It is still a combat among giants, dragons, and cyclopes; the struggle of gods and goddesses, ideas and concepts. The reference to "lived experience" survives in the notes, in the asides. From time to time, Marx illustrates his thought with examples from the real world. Without these illustrations the reader of these sketches would have no idea what the author was talking about, what he was driving at in his writing. This has given the *Manuscripts* their enigmatic and, therefore, stimulating, character. Every reader takes from them what he needs.

This has a curious result. The many considerations recorded by Marx have meaning and scope only in a social context, namely, urban reality. Yet, Marx never speaks of this directly. Only on one or two occasions, although decisively, does he relate the succession of concepts to this context, which is continuously implied.

Feudal property entails a relationship between the land and human beings. The lord carries the name of the land and the land, along with him, is personalized. The serf is an accessory of the land but the heir (the lord's oldest son) also belongs to the land, a local homeland, uniquely circumscribed, which supports the seigneurial family, the seigneurial home, their lineage and vassalage, and their history. The relationships between the feudal context and those who depend on it are transparent. There is no obscure intermediary like money. The political situation, therefore, has a sentimental side. The noble condition of land ownership gives the lord a romantic halo. But it is necessary, Marx states, that this appearance be suppressed. What is the reason for this historical or theoretical necessity? Marx doesn't expound on this point, however. "It is inevitable that this appearance should be abolished and that landed property, which is the root of private property, should be drawn entirely into the orbit of private property and become a commodity."[2] It is therefore necessary that the personal relationship of the owner to his property should change and "that the marriage of interest with the land should take over from the marriage of honor, and that land, like man, should sink to the level of a venal object" (319). It is inevitable that the cynicism of ownership should become manifest, "that immovable property should become mobile and restless monopoly, competition; and that the idle enjoyment of the products of the sweat and blood of other people should become a brisk commerce in the same" (ibid.). What then? Feudalism would disappear. The old adage "*nulle terre sans seigneur*" would give way to the modern saying "money knows no master" (ibid.).

Once industry had achieved sufficient power (as it had in England, Marx adds), it strips the great landowners of their monopoly, putting those lands into competition with landed property abroad, on the world market (grain). In this way, in England, the great landed properties had already lost their individual character to the extent that they too wanted to become money! Isn't it obvious that the town is simultaneously the place, the instrument, the dramatic theater of this gigantic metamorphosis? Where does this transformation occur once it is no longer conceived solely in terms of abstract categories: "property," "exchange," "money"? This is so obvious that Marx doesn't even consider expressing it. Even when he speaks of the extension of landed property to the urban space, that is, the "relationship of rising rents and rising misery" (315), for "a rise in house rent also means a rise in ground rent—the interest on the land on which the house stands" (ibid.).

The same is true when Marx stigmatizes the effective reduction of "man" in general to a machine (286) for production and consumption, the *reduction* of history to economic laws, the reduction of the worker to an abstract activity (289) and a stomach. As the fundamental attack against private property, now a "global historical power," progresses, criticism advances and the process deepens, the urban context becomes obvious. Alienation appears, producing the refinement of needs and the means to satisfy them together with a return to bestial savagery. "Even the need for fresh air ceases to be a need for the worker. Man reverts once more to living in a cave, but the cave is now polluted by the mephitic and pestilential breath of civilization. Moreover, the worker has no more than a precarious right to live in it, for it is for him an alien power that can be daily withdrawn and from which, should he fail to pay, he can be evicted at any time. He actually has to pay for this mortuary" (359). Where is the dwelling of light Prometheus spoke of in Aeschylus? The cloaca of civilization becomes the element (milieu) of life for the worker. "The Irishman has only one need left—the need to *eat,* to eat *potatoes,* and, more precisely, to eat *rotten potatoes,* the worst kind of potatoes" (360). England and France already have a small Ireland in every industrial city. It is almost by accident that Marx comes to mention the background, which for him is nothing more than a sullen decor. When he shows that the world perceived by "man's" senses is nothing more than the work of this "man," that, in this way, "man" reproduces nature by appropriating it, that the apparently "objective" world or the world that is the illusory work of God, results from labor, he mentions neither the city nor even the countryside.

In fact, there is one fragment, as obscure as it is decisive, that contains such a reference. "The *distinction* between capital and land, between profit and ground rent, and the distinction between both and wages, *industry, agriculture,* and *immovable* and *movable* private property is not one which is grounded in the nature of things, it is a *historical* distinction, a *fixed* moment in the formation and development of the opposition between capital and labor" (337). It is decisive because all of Marx's subsequent work, including *Capital,* will be devoted to commenting on this historical situation and showing how it was transformed. The answer comes only at the conclusion of Marx's great (unfinished) work. The elements of capitalist society occur in history, but *outside* each other: land, owners, nature—labor, laborers detached from the means of production—capital, money in search of profit, the capitalist, the bourgeoisie. The workers? They began as vagabonds. Money? It originates in trade. The owner? He was once a lord. Society (bourgeois) takes up these elements, which it receives separately; it develops them, mixes them together, combines them into a unity: expanded production, global surplus labor, surplus value on the scale of an entire society (rather than that of the isolated enterprise, capitalist, or owner). But the old differences reappear; they become partly illusory, partly real. The categories of population, classes, and class segments do not know that they are participating in the production of surplus value, in its realization, its distribution. They continue to see themselves as distinct; the worker believes he receives the price of his labor (salary), the owner withdraws the rent from the ground that belongs to him, and the capitalist the fruit (profit) of his productive capital. Whereas it is simply a question of the redistribution of (global) surplus value! Thus, particular aspects of history are transformed into internal differences in the capitalist mode of production (system), with one part illusion and one part reality, but indistinct. The *separation* of classes is both illusory and real. It is illusory because they are part of the same society, part of the same "whole" that is systematized. Moreover, there is only one source of social wealth. It is real in the sense that these classes exist socially and practically within a separation, maintained as such, that often ends in conflict. Where does this *capital* metamorphosis take place (quite specifically, the metamorphosis that creates capital and capitalism)? In industry and in *city life,* which are formed in opposition to rural ownership, whose traces and stigmata they bear for years to come. It is within the city, therefore, in and through city life, in opposition to nature, to peasant life, to the countryside already shaped by agricultural labor, that a conflict with tremendous consequences unfolds. Property does not achieve its abstract (that is, *private*) essence, inseparable from abstract (that is, *social*) labor, other than by wearing down the immediate, primitive, ownership of land, until its ultimate disappearance. Movable wealth (money, capital) thus supplants natural wealth in land, in the products of the soil. This natural property gives the owner an almost magical prestige. He cannot be "deprived" of it. The aristocrat bore a romantic halo. As a twentieth-century sociologist said, he was marked by charisma. The owner of money, of capital, of shares and bills, has lost this prestige. He has stripped property of its mystical value. But in what context? In city life, the medium (milieu, means, mediation, intermediary) of the transformation. And now the monster has finally been named, the place of metamorphoses and encounters, the theatrical space that blends the illusory and the real, and simulates appropriation (where appropriation in the form of alienation constitutes the "right to the city"), where victorious capital seems to have discovered human labor as a source of wealth.

I'd like to conclude this discussion of the *Economic and Philosophic Manuscripts of 1844*; their importance today should neither be overestimated nor underestimated. Like signposts along a road, the texts supply a direction, a sense of orientation. What they lack and what they reveal are as important as what they provide by what they say. Out of the (dialectical) shock between categories, conceptual clouds and storms hurl lightning bolts, give birth to a new dawn. But to pursue my line of thought, I'd like to set aside any other questions that might be addressed to the Marx of 1844 and turn instead to *The German Ideology* (1845–46).

Was this a result of the direct influence of Engels? Contact with the facts? The landscape has changed. Urban reality comes to the fore, although in a limited way. To situate this appearance of the city in Marxist thought, to understand its importance and limitations, we need to understand the distinction and indissoluble connection between the *division of labor* and *ideology*.

The confrontation between ontology and anthropology (between the old philosophy oriented toward metaphysics and the "physical" position of the human being considered as a being of nature) revealed the radical conflict between those two representations. It is impossible to be satisfied with mere eclecticism, with vague synthesis. Taken to its culmination by Marx with incomparable theoretical force, there is only one way out: resolve the conflict by overcoming it, by breaking the terms of the contradiction with a "theoretical revolution" (the expression is found at the beginning of the *Economic and Philosophic Manuscripts,* and attributed to Hegel and Feuerbach).

Marx and Engels conceptualize a two-sided process: history and praxis. History summarizes the production of the human being by himself. The word *production* here should be understood in a much broader sense than it is understood by economists. It gathers to itself the meaning of philosophy as a whole: the production of things (products) and works, ideas and ideologies, consciousness and knowledge, illusions and truths. Thus, history runs from the distant (original) past to the present and the historian retraces this path to understand how that past was able to engender the present. *Praxis,* on the other hand, based on this movement, supported by the present and constituting it, prepares the future, envisages the possible, that is, ultimately, the complete transformation of the real world through total revolution. Social practice (praxis) is analyzed: production in the limited sense and social productivity, political practice, revolutionary practice, and so on. For Marx, materialist and dialectical thought alone has been able to capture the determining factors of this process— *historicity* and *praxis*—by addressing the complexity, the differences, and the associated conflicts and contradictions. It is this that constitutes *historical materialism*.

There is a problem, however. If this is accurate, if history and praxis are the basis of understanding, how is it that men living in society have taken so long to realize this? How can their relations give rise to illusions and lies while the truth cries out to be heard? Where did the error arise? How can we explain the incredible mixture of delusion and reason in people's heads?

The founders of the new doctrine dismissed "philosophical heroes" but had to avoid being associated with this model. In what does philosophical illusion consist? First, in that, for the philosopher, everything occurs in the realm of pure thought, outside the profane world. Second, in that the philosopher chooses an abstract category—mankind, consciousness, substance, uniqueness—to which he attributes a singular importance, turning it into an absolute. Attempting to be a "critic," he attacks his peers, the "false ideas" accepted by other philosophers, currently accepted religious beliefs. This self-proclaimed revolutionary philosopher believes he is changing the world, whereas he dreams of brushing aside dogmas very much like his own. But his thought is never troubled by one essential question: what are the assumptions, the conditions of existence of that thought? What is the connection between philosophy and the German reality? The philosopher doesn't bother asking. Marx and Engels formulate the question while providing the answer. They do not start with dogmas, or build on arbitrary foundations, but from real foundations: individuals, conditions of existence that can be empirically determined.

It is worth noting that after this statement, the authors of *The German Ideology* jump—a prodigious leap—from the actual to its origins. What is *original* about the activities by which "men" *produce,* directly or indirectly, their conditions by modifying nature? "Production" entails "reproduction," both physical and social: reproduction of a way of life. "Rather it is a definite form of activity of these individuals, a definite form of expressing their life, a definite mode of life on their part. As individuals express their life, so they are. What they are, therefore, coincides with their production, both with what they produce and with how they produce."[3]

Here, a new leap, this time forward. We jump from "human beings" (distinguished from animals by *producing*, by working with instruments invented by them, distinct from their body) to national differences. The critical rereading of famous texts in no way diminishes their importance, but it no longer allows us to overlook the gaps in their arguments. This is the only approach that will enable us to identify their strengths and weaknesses. Robust affirmations, those our memory retains and that result in well-known quotations, do not always coincide with the strengths of their theoretical development. It is all too easy to identify and emphasize faulty propositions that have been unreasonably praised and unjustly underestimated (for example, in this case, the well-known argument that reduces thought and consciousness to a simple "reflection" of outside reality).

Wouldn't the first genuinely concrete point, one not based on an arbitrary temporal overview nor recourse to the original, be the set of propositions concerning the city? The division of labor "within a nation" results in the separation of industrial and commercial labor from agricultural labor. (This is a rather vague statement. Where do these "nations" come from? From the division of labor—an argument that comes close to being tautological.). This results in "the separation of town and country and the conflict of their interests" (38). More generally, this is followed by multiple divisions and particular separations of social activities. There is a connection between the development of the division of labor, the differences between labor and exchange, and the different forms of ownership: initially, communitarian (tribal) property with the gradual predominance of the family and the quasi-natural division of labor within the family, then communal property, which derives from the confluence of several tribes in a *town*, whether by contract or conquest. Alongside this communal property, private property takes shape and develops, but initially as an anomalous form of communal property, primarily, the ownership of slaves.

Here, we discover an opposition between commerce and industry within the town. The argument is quite remarkable for its strength and novelty. The obscurity of the formulation (what exactly does the word *form* mean in the expression "forms of ownership"?) disappears. The authors make a point whose importance the *history of historians* has not always managed to acknowledge in *historicity*, although it is a decisive formulation, a landmark in historical time.

Antiquity began with the city while the Middle Ages (European, Western) began in the countryside. In antiquity, the *political* city organized, dominated, protected, administered, and exploited a territory, with its peasants, villagers, herders, and so on. In a few cases—Athens, Rome—this political city began to dominate, through warfare as much as through exchange (barter and commerce), a territory that was incomparably larger than its immediate environs. At the heart of this urban growth the only major conflict was the one between slaves and citizens. There were no other class relationships.

During the Middle Ages, these relationships were inverted. The lord relied on the countryside; he ruled over a small territory, which he hoped to expand. Feudal property is the result of a two-part process: the breakdown of the Roman Empire (which nonetheless left behind an extensive swath of land under cultivation and vast spaces already united by commercial and political ties) and the arrival of the barbarians, who restored a community, that of the peasants. The hierarchical structure of medieval society had as its base the seigneurs' control of land and the military on territory occupied by dependent communities. Restoration of the community by the barbarians did not reestablish the ancient form of communal ownership, it merely subordinated it to feudal structures. These were directed against *the dominated productive class* (that of the peasants) as well as the *towns* (against their inhabitants, the "bourgeoisie," who engaged in trade and maintained the system of exchange). A two-part *class struggle* arose, in particular the bitter struggle between the bourgeoisie and the feudal lords. This led to the urban revolution of the Middle Ages and the emergence of the royal state.

Where did the economic, social, and political *stagnation* arise that led to the decline of ancient society and its empires? There were several reasons for this: slavery, which limited growth (low productivity and the lack of inventiveness of the slaves), and the fact that there were no significant class struggles other than the vain struggles of slaves against their masters. During the Middle Ages, however, in Europe, the town, which had been subject to a feudal structure, overcame its domination. At the same time, the town destroyed that feudal structure and incorporated it, transforming it in the process.

To the feudal system of land ownership (landed property: peasant communities ruled by the nobility) "there corresponded corporative property in the towns." The community of artisans supported the hierarchy of various masters: corporate masters, the urban oligarchy, wealthy individuals who ruled the city politically. The association of producers struggled against a rapacious nobility, organized markets (covered halls), accommodated the escaped serfs, and ensured the protection and growth of existing small (commercial) capital.

The structure of these two forms (landed property and corporative property in the towns) depended on existing relationships of production and the limited productive forces available: agriculture was still rudimentary, industry still artisanal, exchanges were few, and the division of labor minimal. Ownership was divided among the various "orders": the nobility, the clergy, commoners, or princes, peasants, and skilled craftsmen.

This structure was transformed when the commercial towns grew in size, when the cities began to join together in federations or fight one another for dominance. This brought about a division between trade and industry, on the one hand, and an alliance between the landed nobility and the urban oligarchs, on the other. These events took place only after the victory of the towns over the landed nobility (revolution of the communes and the urban bourgeoisie), that is, the reversal of the initial situation—the dominance of the countryside, landed property, and feudal structures over the still weak towns.

We shouldn't force the ideas found in these texts by Marx and Engels too much; it is sufficient to compare them to other texts (generally written later) to draw certain conclusions from them. Ancient society (a mode of production based on slavery) had dwindled without *producing* another mode of production, another society. Its history was mostly that of its decline, following a short, brilliant period of ascension. The reason for this can be found in the fact that the ancient polis represented a closed system. The internecine struggles could only damage it from within without opening the way to another practical reality. The slave revolts, although highly legitimate, were over before they had even begun. Why? Because domination of the *political city* over the surrounding countryside was a given from the start, was integral to the "town–country" relationship. The use of slaves for agricultural work (on the great estates, the latifundia) was dependent on the polis, which used its means of production and the conditions of its power. The contradiction remained internal to the polis. This relationship forced the ancient polis not only to hit a ceiling, from every point of view, but also to undergo the destructive, self-destructive even, counterattack of struggles that it sustained and contained. The contradictions of the ancient polis did more to destroy than to promote any chance of progress.

During the European Middle Ages, however (carefully setting aside the case of the "Asiatic mode of production"), the relationship between town and country became one of conflict. Following the massive incursion of barbarians, who carried out history's decree against the ancient city and replaced it with a society that was once again tribal and community-based, the medieval town and bourgeoisie had to win the struggle for political supremacy and the ability to economically exploit the countryside, substituting themselves for the landed nobility in drawing off surplus labor (land rent), and in ownership itself (by destroying feudal ownership of the land as part of a long-term process already fore-seen). The *urban system* was unable to form a closed system, for it represented the destruction (opening up) of the *feudal system*. During this process, the town engendered something different and greater than itself. Economically, it created industry; socially, it created movable property (not without compromising with feu-dal forms of ownership and organization); politically, it created the state. This was the historical result of the first great struggle in Europe of classes and social forms: town against countryside, bourgeoisie against the feudal nobility, movable and private prop-erty against landed and community-based property.

Here, the reader will note that in *The German Ideology*, a first development in the relationship between town and country is in-terjected between its fundamental propositions (philosophical criticism of philosophy) and a new series of general propositions, clearly defining "historical materialism." How can we fail to con-clude that the historical materialism presented by Marx and En-gels does not consist of philosophical generalities (although di-rected against philosophers) but relies on a history that had been neglected until then (and perhaps until today), namely, that of the city?

"Here are the facts." Particular individuals enter into particular social and political relations (which they maintain in their prac-tice, which they "make" but which do not depend on them, which they have not chosen). The connection between the sociopolitical structure and production can be observed, demonstrated. "The social structure and the state are continually evolving out of the life-process of definite individuals, however, of these individuals, not as they may appear in their own or other people's imagina-tion, but as they *actually* are; i.e. as they act, produce materially, and hence as they work under definite material limits, presuppo-sitions and conditions independent of their will" (41).

A key formulation is presented at this point. What is *produc-tion*? In the broad sense, inherited from Hegel but transformed by the critique of philosophy in general, that of Hegelianism in particular, and by the contributions of anthropology, production is not limited to activity, which manufactures things for exchange. There are works and there are products. Production in this broad sense (production of the human being) implies and comprises that of ideas, representations, language. It is intimately connected to "material activity and the material intercourse of men—the language of real life" (42). Men produce representations and ideas, but these are "real, active men."

There is nothing, therefore, outside production, nothing human. The mental, the intellectual, whatever passes as "spiritual," and what philosophy takes to be its intrinsic domain are "products" just like the rest. We can produce representations, ideas, and truths as easily as illusions and errors. We can produce consciousness itself, which a remarkable fragment confirms and expands: "The mind is from the outset afflicted with the curse of being 'burdened' with matter, which here makes its appearance in the form of agitated layers of air, sounds, in short, of language. Language is as old as consciousness, language *is* practical, real consciousness that exists for other men as well, and only therefore does it also exist for me; language, like consciousness, only arises from the need, the necessity of intercourse with other men" (49). For Marx and Engels, there can be no thought without consciousness and no consciousness without language, that is to say, without support and without relationships. The human being is distinguished from the biological creature in that he creates his relationships and, as a result, possesses a language: his language, with which relationships exist as relationships. Consciousness, therefore, is a (social) product. As for "self-consciousness," which would exist by itself, the absolute form of consciousness, mind, divinity, it is an illusion of philosophers. It is worth pointing out in passing that we could also put together a collection of Marx's texts on the subject of language. Although he never developed his ideas about language and would no doubt have lacked the conceptual tools, he appears to sketch out an approach to the question (for example, with respect to the relation between language and exchange value).

Philosophy has come down from heaven to earth; materialist thought rises from the earth to the heavens. It originates with the actual activity of mankind. It is not consciousness that determines (social) life but life that determines consciousness. Freedom is a "historical not an intellectual fact . . . men must be in a position to live in order to be able to 'make history.' But life involves before everything else eating and drinking, housing, clothing, and various other things. The first historical act is thus the production of the means to satisfy these needs, the production of material life itself" (47).

It is not my aim here to follow the construction of historical materialism but to situate within that development the theoretical fragments and ideas of Marx and Engels concerning the city. Therefore, I will bypass the section on "History" but would like to add a few remarks concerning the way Engels and Marx play with the two senses of the word *production*.

a) The commonly accepted view, inherited from philosophy. Here, *production* signifies *creation* and applies to the arts, sciences, institutions, and the state itself, as it does to what are generally referred to as "practical" activities. The division of labor, which fragments production and causes the process to escape consciousness, is also a production, as are consciousness and language. Nature, which is itself transformed, is a product; the world of the senses, which appears to be a given, is created.

b) The narrow, precise, sense inherited from economists (Adam Smith, David Ricardo), although reduced and reductive, is modified by the contribution of a comprehensive worldview: history.

Marx and Engels approach the nature of production in two ways. To the broad (philosophical or quasi-philosophical) but vague use of the term "production" they add a precise, empirical, almost "positive" sense associated with its narrow use. They correct the narrow sense (reduced and reductive) of this last use by projecting into it the scope and broad perspective of its other meaning. In the broad sense, we have the production of works, of ideas, of apparent "spirituality," of everything that makes a society and a civilization. In the narrow sense, we have the *production* of goods—food, clothing, housing, things. The latter sense supports the first and identifies its material "foundation."

Marx and Engels succeed in convincing the reader that history comprises and contains this twofold process, this twofold sense. However, their argument is beset by a degree of disorder, by structural weaknesses that might explain why the authors abandoned their work, which they never published. They again return to the question of origins to examine the "four aspects of the original historical relations," namely, the production of means (instruments, tools) used to satisfy the first need—the production of new needs—reproduction, that is, the family—the links that connect workers during production. Four "moments" that are both original and perpetual, which is to say, historical. It is clear that these "moments," being inherent to *all* history, say nothing about what history was and is. History is introduced with the division of labor, which assumes its character only with the appearance of the division of material and intellectual labor. "From this moment onwards consciousness *can* really flatter itself that it is something other than the consciousness of existing practices, that it really represents something without representing something real" (50). Having said this, the authors jump from the analysis of "moments" to actual considerations of national consciousness and national (German) pretentions to universal consciousness. These are excellent critical considerations but they overshoot their premises by leaping over history in the name of history. The remaining argument suffers from this somewhat overly dialectical leap, especially the considerations that return to the philosophical theory of alienation in the name of history, without indicating whether it is a question of alienation or disalienation by history! Why should

criticism spare critical thought? In fact, the text resumes its coherence and scope, and its interest grows, once we return to the
town (84ff.). It is as if the town effectively and concretely reunited
both meanings of the central term "production."

This section picks up the arguments of the earlier remarks
about the town but on a higher level. Between the two, what do
we have? Insights into historical development and its wealth, insights that are rich in stimulating expressions but mix ideas taken
from every era, from the origins of civilization to total revolution.
How we have wandered (notwithstanding the occasional return)
from the man who served as the pretext and namesake of the argument: Feuerbach. Such opulent confusion! Generations of exegetes have attempted to introduce order, method, and rigor, but
have contented themselves with picking from this mother lode a
handful of quotations, always the same.

With this second fragment on the city, their thinking once
again becomes dense, chronologically precise, and clearly situated. The return to earlier themes provides them with new material and a concentrated form. At times the modern reader has the
impression that Marx and Engels have the answer to a question
that lingers at the tip of their pen: "What is the subject of history?"
For them, in these pages, the subject of history is the city. I don't
want to jump to conclusions, though. Marx does get around to the
question of the "subject" but it is only made explicit in the *Grundrisse*. The collective subject, that of history, the general subject,
praxis as a whole, is no longer the Hegelian state; Marx refuted it
in his critique of Hegelianism (the philosophy of history and the
history of philosophy, the theory of the state and of law). What
then? Marx hesitates in providing a definitive answer. Is it "society"? The mode of production? Classes? The proletariat as the
privileged class, negatively and positively? Possibly considering
the question itself as speculative (philosophical and not practical
or political), it appears that Marx declines to provide an answer,
although the question has been presented clearly and distinctly.

Here, the subject of history is unquestionably the city; it is introduced with specific characteristics.

a) The countryside, unlike the town, is dispersed and isolated. The town *concentrates* not only the populace but the instruments of production, capital, needs, pleasures. That is why "The advent of the town implies, at the same time, the necessity of administration, police, taxes, etc., in short, of the municipality *[des Gemeindewesens],* and thus of politics in general" (72).

Urban existence is conflated with political existence, as the word indicates. If the town concentrates that which is needed to create a society, it distributes it in a relatively reasonable way in the form of organizations and institutions.

b) Nevertheless, the separation between town and country mutilates and impedes the social totality; it depends on the material and intellectual division of labor it embodies and projects across the land. In this separation, it is the countryside's responsibility to provide material labor devoid of intelligence and the city's responsibility to provide a form of labor enriched and developed by the intellect, including the functions of administration and control. This rift is deepened by the immense social progress that transpires: the transition from barbarism to civilization, from tribal organization to the state, from provincialism to the nation. It is the initial and perpetual moment of history, which persists "through the whole history of civilization to the present day" (ibid.). But this is the negative side of history, the bad side by which it advances. The separation brings with it the separation of the population into classes. This separation "can only exist within the framework of private property," that of the land and money, with the substitution of one for the other as the dominant power. This results in generalized alienation. The individual subordinated to the division of labor experiences an activity and a situation that have been imposed on him. His "hominization" (a word that postdates Marx and Engels but has a theoretical relevance here) is curtailed. He regresses to the prehistoric level.

On one side we have the "rural-animal" and on the other side the "town-animal," both of them limited. Are Marx and Engels here referring to a celebrated fable? One of the equally well-known fragments of Hegel's *Phenomenology* discusses abstract animals: specialists mutilated by the division of labor, both in the abstract sense and in their reduction to the biological. One does not preclude the other. This imposes two sets of limits: that of life and consciousness, that of practical activity and creative ability. The benefits of the town are turned against it. There is an antagonism between the interests of the urban animal and those of the animal of the fields. Their hatreds and struggles would be in vain if they didn't *produce* another society.

c) The separation of town and country can and must be overcome, as must the division of labor itself. (Later, especially in the *Grundrisse*, Marx showed how this overcoming, whose inspiration was taken from relatively undivided agricultural labor, and from utopians like Fourier, who theorized agrarian community life, reached a higher meaning through industrial labor and automation.) The abolition of the contradictions between town and country "is one of the first conditions of communal life" (ibid.). That is to say, communal life once it has been resumed following a period of historical development, together with its conquests, in so-called communist society. This overcoming results in a "mass of material premises, which cannot be fulfilled by the mere will" (ibid.) and, more specifically, the growth of productive forces as well as new relations of production (and consequently another mode of production, another society). Therefore, this overcoming does not result from a decree, an intention of consciousness. There is a *trend in this direction, it is the direction of the trend of history,* that of practice and society as a whole, which, in this way, is made explicit.

Consequently, the town clearly encompasses both senses of "production." Itself a work, it is the site where various works are produced, including those that guide the direction of production: needs and enjoyments. It is also the place where goods are produced and exchanged, and where they are consumed. It consolidates these realities, these modalities of "production," some of which are immediate and some of which are mediate (indirect). It concretizes this unity, for which it is the social support, the "subject," and dates it, while the town itself remains abstract and undated.

From this perspective, the return at a higher level to the claims made about the medieval city provides much greater force to their argument. The towns produced the bourgeoisie as well as the first proletarians. To better understand this, we can examine the division of labor. It appears that divided forms of labor complete one another; their results are interconnected because they are mutually necessary. If a group, organized or not, produces instruments, the group that makes use of them is indispensable to the society. Therefore, it would appear that the division of labor replaces a simple society with a more complex, more harmonious, more "organic" society, as Durkheim would have it. But Marx says that this is not the case. The results, the "products" complement each other but the divided activities are antagonistic, bringing about inequality and conflict.

Let us consider, in the first stage of social life—tribal or communal society—divided labor in the extended family primarily along age and sex lines. Of course, they are interconnected, they assume each other's presence and complement one another. In a small number of cases, they provide women with a status of honor, an important role. And yet, in the great majority of known cases, the status of women deteriorates. Men dominate; they deprecate women's activities or relegate women to deprecated activities. The inequality of functions leads to the struggle between the sexes and those conditions prevail in spite of all the reasons and causes that maintain the unity of the sexes within social groups: sentiments, desires, religion, morality, rites, and so on. The inequality of the sexes, consequently, and their struggle are inherent to the family. The equality of the sexes is an empty word, a vaporous claim, even on the economic level, without considering the suppression of the family. Are there social units that are chained (bound) to each other by a rational connection, in which work is strictly complementary? Marx claims that there are: in the *enterprise* and only in the enterprise. Here, there reigns a *technical division* of labor. Under this division of labor, the instruments of labor are in control and create an interdependence. The technical division of labor differs profoundly from the social division. To the extent that where a technical division exists, there is unity and solidarity, complexity and complementarity. The separation of functions into those of control and production is a social, not a technical, fact. In the capitalist mode of production, the social division of labor occurs in the market, based on market requirements and the risks it entails. There is none of the rationality that may apply to the enterprise. In the market, there is competition and, therefore, the possibility of conflicts followed by actual conflicts, between individuals, groups, classes.

Within a production unit such as the enterprise, there is a division of labor between the workshops and other parts of the enterprise, and among the productive individuals within the workshop.

In this sense, we may very well ask if, during and after the Middle Ages, there didn't exist a technical division of labor within the town that turned it into a type of giant enterprise or workshop, given the dispersion of productive units throughout the countryside. We might seek out the relationship in the guild between a certain technical division of labor, which was very weak, and a very powerful social division, which had already been formed as a result of market forces. And finally, we might ask about the division of labor between the guilds and the towns themselves. This is what Marx and Engels did in *The German Ideology*, but always subordinated to labor's complementary position with respect to the antagonistic nature of relationships as a whole.

The division of labor, in connection with the forms of ownership, gives rise not only to the social unit but to rivalries and conflicts within society as well. To the already well-known fact that the totality, as such, escapes those who occupy a fixed place

in the whole and have only a limited degree of activity is added
the confrontation between functions. Do town and country complement one another? Yes, in a sense. But, in another sense, the
rivalry between them was inevitable; in the Middle Ages it was
perpetual but fecund, and carried out on various fronts. The in-
flux of fugitive serfs, persecuted by their lords, their continuous
exodus into the chartered towns, which accepted but exploited
them, was an economic form of the conflict whose political form
was the urban military force. Confronted by the territorial nobility as well as the peasants from whom they drew their subsistence and their raw materials (wheat, wool), the towns protected
and organized themselves on both the economic and the political
level: guilds, militias, shared buildings, and so on. Consequently,
this form of organization of the town, directed against an outside adversary, not only had a hierarchy intrinsic to the polis, it
brought about modalities of productive labor destined for a great
future (of course, those who were immediately involved were not
aware of this). The serfs, freed by their entrance into the urban
community, were unable to defend themselves. They arrived one
by one and, therefore, were at the mercy of the guild masters and
stewards. In this way an unorganized mass of day laborers was
formed for whom labor was already being measured in terms of
time (73–74).

Corporative associations in the towns (communitarian and
hierarchical) were multiplied: internally, within the medieval
city-states; externally, among the towns as political entities. These
associations had multiple goals: protecting property and their
members' physical well-being, multiplying the means of production. Effective both economically and politically, they tightly
coupled the two domains. They aimed simultaneously at the rabble inside the town and their adversaries outside—the lords and
princes, as well as the peasants. The revolts of the rabble and
the "journeymen" against the guilds and the municipality rarely
reached the stage of outright rebellion and most often remained
within the guilds themselves. "The great risings of the Middle

Ages all radiated from the country, but equally remained totally ineffective because of the isolation and consequent crudity of the peasants" (74).

In these towns, there was money, merchandise, and markets, in other words, *capital*. But it was not yet capitalism. Marx and Engels explain that the reason for this can be traced to the still spontaneous and natural character of an already highly complex process.

The (dialectical) conflict between town and country does not exclude a certain unity. Rather, as with every dialectical process, it incorporates it. This poses a difficulty for analysis: grasping the exact relationship between unity and contradiction, the moment when difference arises, when it gives way to conflict, when the conflict is resolved (either by creating new differences or by sliding slowly into indifference). *The order of the towns,* which brought about their cohesion, and *the order in the towns,* that of the dominant "bourgeoisie" and the guilds, thus appear as a unit to the landed nobility. *Their* conditions of existence (movable property, artisanal labor) had been latent for a long time before being separated from feudal social arrangements. Even when their differences were acknowledged, *they* assumed the underlying *form. This* form is precisely their *order* (in opposition to the "class"). In the feudal order, membership in a class remains hidden, just as the difference between the person and the group, between the life of the individual and the conditions to which that life is subordinated, is neither perceived nor experienced as such. *Everything appears to be a part of nature and natural.* "In the estate (and even more in the tribe) this is as yet concealed: for instance, a nobleman always remains a nobleman, a commoner always a commoner, apart from his other relationships, a quality inseparable from his individuality" (87), especially the money he does or does not possess. These qualities cannot be separated from individuality. The difference between the "personal" individual and the individual as a member of a class will only appear much later with the growth of competition and the struggle of individuals within bourgeois society. "Thus, in imagination, individuals seem freer under the dominance of the bourgeoisie than before, because their conditions of life seem accidental; in reality, of course, they are less free, because they are to a greater extent governed by material forces" (ibid.). In philosophical terms, they are much more alienated.

"Capital in these towns was a naturally derived capital" (74). It was largely inherited: a house, tools, customers. It was transmitted from father to son as a result of the immature state of exchange and the lack of circulation of goods and money. How could such goods be realized as money, as exchange value? "Unlike modern capital, which can be assessed in money and which may be indifferently invested in this thing or that, this capital was directly connected with the particular work of the owner, inseparable from it and to this extent estate capital" (ibid.) (simultaneously a skill and an order).

There was no division of labor between isolated workers. A guild bore no similarity to a factory floor. Strictly speaking, the technical division of labor only appears in manufacturing. Inside the guilds, each workman "had to be versed in a whole round of tasks, had to be able to make everything that was to be made with his tools" (ibid.). In the narrow context of the medieval city, the artisan rose to a position of artistry. "Every medieval craftsman was completely absorbed in his work, to which he had a complacent, servile relationship, and in which he was subjected to a far greater extent than the modern worker, whose work is a matter of indifference to him" (ibid.).

There is nothing romantic about these texts. What's more, they dissipate romantic illusions concerning the medieval past. We may even wonder whether they don't go too far. Is the modern worker indifferent to work, to his own work? Is it merely a way to earn a living? Although this assumption may be true for some, is it true for all? And why, if true, has the proud dignity of the worker and work, the attachment of the first to the second, been so often and so forcefully affirmed in "socialist" thought? Marx and Engels, here and elsewhere, do not allude to political conditions or "society" as a whole, to the mode of production as a totality. It is a question of the immediate relationship between the worker and his work. An immediate relationship of affective involvement has disappeared, giving way to indifference. And this has occurred because of the division of labor, inherent in the relationships of production and independent of society's higher (superstructural) institutions.

Whatever the case with the medieval city, there is capital without capitalism and workers without a proletariat (even though the "people" or rabble in the towns contain its germ). The reason for this can be found in the fact that we do not find *abstract capital,* a realized abstraction, arising from a specific mode of production, on one side, and *abstract labor,* simultaneously general and circumscribed, indifferent to the worker, on the other. As noted above, we remain on the natural plane, limited to direct, personal, immediate relationships. A certain threshold of social abstraction has not been crossed.

We move a step closer to this threshold when trade is separated from production and a specific class of tradesmen is formed. This implies broader interactions in the towns, which overflow the surrounding countryside, as well as new needs, "whose historical development was determined, in each case, by the degree of culture." If we examine this last formulation, we find that it is not a matter of the advancement of *productive forces,* that is, production in the narrow sense, but of production in the broad sense. New needs arise in those lands accessible to commerce; connections, communications, and means of communication follow. But where do these needs come from? To whom can we attribute them and why?

In short, the various struggles between the town and rural landowners, peasant communities, and the seigneurial class, notwithstanding the immediate relationships that bound them, did not cut the umbilical cord. In the struggle between men joined together against nature, during the course of which those men extended nature while gradually controlling it, the medieval town represents a nodal point, a privileged site. It is no longer "nature" and yet it continues to be. The move toward the abstraction of relationships (an abstraction carried out in practice by the power of money and the division of labor) and toward the facticity of needs followed its course, but this liberation (which contains more than one "negative" aspect) is far from being fully realized. Capitalism strides forward but is not there yet. With the medieval town, we are in a preparatory stage: that of primitive accumulation, the accumulation of wealth, technology, labor, markets, places and territories, communications, and so on. The concept of *accumulation* is not yet clearly identified by Marx. But it is there, quite close. The town is its privileged location and is directly referred to as such.

Marx and Engels highlight the associative capacity of the medieval towns, which was quite remarkable. We have seen how these associations (guilds for the most part) in the towns, were directed sometimes against the rabble, sometimes against the peasantry, sometimes against the territorial lords, and frequently against all of these partners and adversaries. This ability extended outward to other towns, especially when merchants became established as a "special class." At that point, the towns escaped their isolation and cultivated relationships with each other. A division of labor then arises among the towns, "each of which is soon exploiting a predominant branch of industry" (75). Clearly, this represents a social division of labor, controlled by the market and its extension.

These urban associations had tremendous consequences. Together with the products traded, knowledge, technology, and inventions of all kinds were also exchanged along the roads and channels of communication. War or invasion was no longer capable of leveling a country that possessed advanced productive forces and needs. "Only when intercourse has become world intercourse and has as its basis large-scale industry, when all nations are drawn into the competitive struggle, is the permanence

of the acquired productive forces assured" (76). The urban associations of the Middle Ages were a decisive step along this path.

The first consequence of this is the birth of manufacturing,
the initial disruption of the guild system inherent to the medieval town. The manufacturers required a series of conditions—
technology first of all, knowledge, an expanded market, and especially the concentration of people and capital. How and where
did manufacturing arise? Contrary to what we might think, it did
not arise in the *existing town*, even though it required conditions
that were realized by and in the town. According to Marx and Engels, it arose in relation to the "town-country" rather than either
of these terms taken in isolation. The artisan of the towns, closely
bound by the regulations of the guild, had access to a very limited
range of tools; the carpenter, the cabinetmaker, the cobbler han-
dled their tools with skill, just like the stonecutter or smithy, who
was capable of making weapons. None of them used a *machine*.
But the peasants who practiced weaving in the countryside employed a rudimentary but technically capable machine. Nascent
capitalism was able to take control of this technology and provide
weaving with a force that connected it with its initiators. It became and remained the principal manufacturing activity, based
on extensive commercial relations, intensified demand, and the
growing accumulation and mobilization of primitive capital. In
this way was formed, outside the towns and near the villagers who
wove to supply their own needs, a class of weavers whose output
was sold on the markets (inside or outside the town). In these villages and market centers, when the guilds did not paralyze this
extension of productive forces, weaving led to such wealth that
many of them became new towns, and among the most flour-
ishing. Manufacturing, thus freed from the guild, increased the
available mass of capital. "At the same time, manufacture became
a refuge of the peasants from the guilds which excluded them or
paid them badly, just as earlier the guild-towns had served the
peasants as a refuge from the landlords" (77). This led to changes
in the relationship between town and country, as it did in the

relationship between employer and worker, which remained patriarchal in the countryside and small towns but evolved into monetary relationships in the manufacturing cities.

In this way, the medieval town, with its guild system, broke apart and was superseded. The conflict between town and country created something new, however. At nearly the same time, there arose capitalism and the world market, the nation and the state, the bourgeoisie and the proletariat. Of course, given the enormity of the process, many elements and conditions other than the movement inherent in the dialectical relationship between town and country were required. Among them the discovery of America and the maritime route to the Indies, the arrival of gold and colonization, the adventures of the conquistadors and the protective measures taken by states in favor of their manufacturing interests, competition and its limitations. Under these interrelated conditions, the "commercial towns, particularly the maritime towns, became to some extent civilized and acquired the outlook of the big bourgeoisie, but in the factory towns an extreme petty-bourgeois outlook persisted" (80). These events occurred, for the most part, during the eighteenth century.

There is no need to follow the theoretical genesis of capitalism, which holds few surprises (for, in this work, Feuerbach and "critical" philosophy in Germany are the issue at hand). Of course, there is the question of historical materialism as the destruction of ideologies and, consequently, of official philosophy as well as political economy. Yet, does the genesis of capitalism out of concepts and categories, such as the division of labor and the relationship between town and country, does this theoretical genesis coincide with history? The undeniable historical facts that are part of this genesis reveal the abstract fabric engendered by these concepts. However, this also raises new questions. We must assume that later works, including *Capital,* will answer these questions or attempt to do so.

With respect to the town, it does seem that for Marx and Engels it played a pivotal historical role, but only by surpassing itself.

Its associative capabilities, part of the movement that connects it to the countryside (and brings about its antagonism toward the countryside), engender a process that will ultimately lead to large-scale industrial manufacture.

This process universalized competition, transformed all capital into industrial capital, and accelerated the circulation and centralization of that capital. "By universal competition it forced all individuals to strain their energy to the utmost. It destroyed as far as possible ideology, religion, morality, etc. and where it could not do this, made them into a palpable lie. It produced world history for the first time, insofar as it made all civilized nations and every individual member of them dependent for the satisfaction of their wants on the whole world, thus destroying the former natural exclusiveness of separate nations" (81). In other words, large-scale industry resulted in the disappearance of the natural world; its aggressiveness toward nature was without limit, which raises further questions. Was the umbilical cord that bound associated "men" (in conflict) to their origin finally severed? Large-scale industry made science and nature subservient to capital, "and took from the division of labor the last semblance of its natural character"; it succeeded in dissolving all natural relations and turned them into monetary relations. "In the place of naturally grown towns it created modern, large industrial cities, which have sprung up overnight" (82). We note the metaphor, which borrowed from nature the expression of its destruction.

The associative capacity of the town, which had created this process, and through which it surpassed itself and destroyed its initial naturalness, arose from the *relations of production*. Not from productive forces, not from superstructures (religion, ethics, and so on) or ideology, not even from the feudal "mode of production" as such.

In effect, this capacity appeared as a destructive contradiction within medieval society. The "mode of production," to the extent that it succeeded in taking shape, along with its functions and structures, to the extent that theoretical thought was able to conceptualize it as a whole, implies a *hierarchy* (both strict and multiple: the orders, the nobility, the clergy) that makes use of conflictual relations (between peasants and lords, between lords and the bourgeoisie, between princes and kings, between the emerging state and its "subjects") while *destroying* them. The relation between town and country resists this destruction and, consequently, leads to the collapse of a powerful sociopolitical architecture. The associative character inherent in the town ultimately spreads to the countryside, brings about new forms that rise above it. It triumphed—although not without a struggle—against the hierarchization inherent in feudalism and against the never-ending conflicts (those of the peasants against the nobility, among others). The mode of production, as a totality, comprised an essential or principal contradiction, one that was destructive but dynamic because it concentrated and resolved other conflicts. This contradiction was more powerful than the one that existed initially between serfs and their feudal landowners, between peasants and the nobility.

With the appearance of large-scale industry, the town (and its internal–external capacity for association, concentration, and assembly) ceased to be a "subject" of the historical process for Marx and Engels. The transition to capitalism, where the town is the social support and vehicle, would present the problem of the subject in a new light (and perhaps cause it to disappear).

Is that all there is to be said about the town? Hardly. In the social and economic contexts that result from the process, within the capitalist mode of production, the town persists: industrial cities, commercial cities, political cities. Nor did the relationship between town and country disappear on the world scale. So what happened to the town? We'll return to this later but, for now, with respect to *The German Ideology*, Marx and Engels simply sketch the broad outlines. Their proposition is not without importance or interest, even though it is introduced somewhat abruptly. For, in this work, it is a question of nothing less than the *end of the town*.

Large-scale industry brought about a *separate economy*. The predominance of the economic characterizes capitalism; with it, the division of labor, competition, market, and productive requirements become limiting factors. The power of industry weighs on individuals, on workers, on all of society. The process that separates the economic from the social and enables politics to thrive while maintaining this separation reaches far back in time. What can we do, today, to do away with the separate economy? Yes, we would have to eliminate private property, but that is not the only condition. We would also have to abolish the division of labor and political institutions. We would have to form a "shared economy" on a practical, *associative* basis (and not only on an ideological basis, as in the religious orders). But this revolution assumes, on the one hand, the simultaneous suppression of the town and the countryside and, on the other hand, the generalization of the activity of urban agglomerations, where communal structures have been built, including those built for specific purposes (barracks, prisons, and so on).

It is remarkable and paradoxical that, in 1845, Marx and Engels found the town to be both an obstacle to the new society they projected and its prototype. And in a very concrete way. The use of productive forces in the urban context—water conduits, lighting, steam heat—all indicate a path toward communal organization. Nor was this merely a question of domestic economy. "That the supersession of individual economy is inseparable from the supersession of the family is self-evident" (84). We can only admire in this passage the remark that this is "self-evident." The critique of political economy, when taken to its logical conclusion, begins to resemble the radical critique of the state, the family, religion, philosophy, ideology, and so on. The role of the town, however, remains ambiguous, even contradictory: the town will end but the "urban" will be promoted, or established or restored on a worldwide scale.

Curiously, Marx and Engels didn't explore the town as a place of birth, the social context and condition of a succession of ideologies and forms of knowledge: reason and rationality, science and scientificity, philosophy and speculation. In a work that concerns itself with ideology, on this important point they are satisfied with a handful of scattered observations. Would the theoretical and ideological capacity of the town have been so inferior to its associative capacity, to its influence as a place of greater interaction and density? No less curiously, the hundreds of pages devoted to Stirner in *The German Ideology* barely allude to this context and these social conditions. No doubt because the author of *The Ego and Its Own* rarely alludes to the subject. The unique individual unfolds within an absolute, which is only attached, for better or worse, to a history: to his history, which has nothing in common with that of his "empirical" conditions. The Unique Individual—the Stirnerian individual—has no urban properties.

For Marx and Engels, the enormous repressive power, which is omnipresent and extends as far as a consciousness (Stirner's among others) that believes it can set itself free, can and must destroy itself during a patient, long-term endeavor that will replace the powers of enslavement with the capacity for freedom. If there is a leap, it is not here, in the actual. Its conditions are not realized; Stirner's "All or nothing," his "All and right now," contain the worst absurdity. To abolish the division of labor implies overcoming it rather than denying it and taking a step backward toward the archaic, the primitive, that is, a domestic community deprived of its definition, its organization, its institution, its structure, namely, *the family.* A family without a family, communism without community, a return to pre-urban society—that is how Stirner's project is defined (see *The German Ideology* and the fragment on Fourier used to attack utopian socialism).

What is referred to as "Marxist" theory takes a great step forward with *The Poverty of Philosophy* (1847). This time Marx attacks Proudhon, in whom he identifies a series of misunderstandings and errors concerning the division of labor and dialectics. Proudhon, who saw himself as a methodical dialectician, distinguishes the "good side" and the "bad side" of things and people. In contemporary society, he wants to promote the good by rejecting the bad. However, "it is the bad side that produces the movement which makes history, by providing a struggle."[4] Had there been economists during the feudal period, they would have been overcome by considerable enthusiasm for the chivalric virtues, the harmony between rights and duties, patriarchal life in the towns, the prosperity of domestic industry in the countryside, the grandeur of urban industry organized by the guilds and their masters. They would have proposed eliminating anything that cast a shadow on this picture: serfdom, privileges (those of the nobles and clergy primarily but also the nascent bourgeoisie), anarchy. And the result? "All the elements which called forth the struggle would have been annihilated, and the development of the bourgeoisie would have been stifled in the germ" (89).

In principle, Marx writes, "a porter differs less from a philosopher than a mastiff from a greyhound. It is the division of labor which has placed an abyss between the two" (94). Proudhon sees a good and bad side to the division of labor. He reproaches the economists for having insisted on the advantages; he will demonstrate the inconveniences. But he understands nothing of the division of labor. He examines it from its smallest side, on the scale of the workshop or the individual worker, or simply from the vantage point of the literal understanding of the word *divide*. Its *comprehensive* aspect escapes him. "Certainly, things would be made much too easy if they were reduced to M. Proudhon's categories. History does not proceed so categorically. Three whole centuries have been necessary in Germany to establish the first great division of labor—that is, the separation of the town from the country. As this single relation, that of town and country, became modified, so the whole society was modified in consequence. . . . The extent of the market, and its physiognomy, give to the division of labor in the different epochs a physiognomy, a character, which it would be difficult to deduce from the single word division, from the idea, or from the category" (ibid.).

Proudhon's confusion consists in the abstract and tautological identification of the *technical division* of labor with the *social division* of labor. He takes the *machine* and the *workshop*, which he confuses, to be *social* categories. For Proudhon, machines are the logical antithesis of the division of labor; his dialectics transforms machinery into workshops. "After presupposing the modern workshop, in order to make poverty the outcome of the division of labor, Monsieur Proudhon presupposes poverty engendered by the division of labor, in order to come to the workshop and be able to represent it as the dialectic negation of that poverty" (97). Excellent dialectics, continues Marx, who draws from these objections a skepticism of the method.

"Machinery is no more an economic category than the bullock that drags the plough. Machinery is merely a productive force. The modern workshop, which depends on the application of machinery, is a social production relation, an economic category" (ibid.). Serious consequences result from Proudhon's misunderstanding. "Society as a whole has this in common with the interior of a workshop, that it too has its division of labor. If one took as a model the division of labor in a modern workshop, in order to apply it to a whole society, the society best organized for the production of wealth would undoubtedly be that which had a single chief employer, distributing tasks to the different members of the community according to a previously fixed rule. But this is by no means the case. While inside the modern workshop, the division of labor is meticulously regulated by the authority of the employer, modern society has no other rule, no other authority, for the distribution of labor than free competition" (99).

This is a remarkable fragment. Let's set aside the element of bad faith in this attack on Proudhon, whom he reproaches for certain implications of his doctrine, which Proudhon would have rejected with the greatest horror. It is true that for Marx, intentions and subjectivity counted little alongside implications and consequences. But it is no less true that Proudhon survived these attacks, which were intended to destroy him. Proudhon is no theoretical cadaver, any more than Stirner, today. But what is important is that Marx has identified the *project* that would later emerge from capitalist society during the transformations of competition and simultaneously provide a model for socialism and neocapitalism. To treat society as a whole as a workshop, to identify the social division of labor and the technical division of labor, and thus organize the production of wealth, to subject the members of a society (classes as well as social groups) to a predetermined rule was initially the product of a brilliant imagination and then a program justified by a "historical and descriptive" methodology, as Marx ironically remarks.

Such a project might encounter certain obstacles, however, the internal and external contradictions of that society, for example. This is as true today as it was in Marx's day, and this is what Marx is analyzing. The market, especially the global market, with its requirements and laws, cannot be *reduced* to the organization of the enterprise (the workshop). The same holds true for town and country, their separation and conflicts. Only ideologues are able to tautologically identify in the term "divide" the technical division of labor and the social division of labor, or to conceive of one through simple analogy with the other. They are different, however, and the conflicts between them will remain inevitable as long as the division of labor is not overcome.

But the division of labor cannot overcome this reduction. On the contrary, it aggravates it. Proudhon believed that the workshop, a collection of machines, abolished the social division of labor through technology. But this was a terrible error. The machine is an assemblage of instruments, not at all a combination of tasks for the worker. "Simple tools, accumulation of tools; composite tools; the setting in motion of a composite tool by a single hand engine, by man; the setting in motion of these instruments by natural forces, machines; system of machines having one motor; system of machines having an automatic motor—this is the progress of machinery" (101), writes Marx, citing Babbage, the theoretician of automated machinery. The meaning and end of the machine is comprehensive automation. This is not without its contradictions, of course. The path to automation is strewn with the sufferings of workers and the resistance of the proletariat to the "incipient domination of the automaton" (103). But the issue, the solution, is approached from the bad side: extreme division, the extreme subdivision of work imposed by technology and the market, by competition and monopolies. How can the now unbearable division of labor be ended once and for all? By the end of work. By nonwork!

Returning to these hypotheses and taking them to their logical conclusion, namely, the elaboration of a theoretical concept, Marx will later write in the *Grundrisse* that nature constructs neither machines nor automated devices (a formula that is a bit too far-reaching today, and to which certain reservations would apply). Automated devices are *products* of human thought and will act on and in nature. Not only that, for they are "organs of the brain," created by the human hand, "objective scientific energy." Their existence shows that social knowledge and knowledge in general have become *immediate* productive forces and that, as a result, the conditions of the process of social life have "fallen under the control of the intellect." At this level, the productive forces of society are not only produced according to a distinct plan, that of knowledge, and then put into practice; they are the "immediate organs of social practice."

The scientific analysis and application of mechanical and chemical laws allow work that would once have been carried out by workers to be accomplished automatically. This occurs only when large-scale industry reaches a higher level, when "all the sciences are prisoners of capital" and existing machinery offers great possibilities. Here, the application of science to production is determinant. Yet, development is not carried out in this manner. *The way forward is the analysis,* that is, the *division of labor,* which is used to substitute a mechanism for labor because labor has been transformed into a mechanism. "What had been the activity of the worker became the activity of the machine," so that the absorption of labor by capital rose up suddenly to confront the worker. The automated system is merely the realized form of mechanization. "Set in motion by an automaton, a moving power that moves itself; the automaton consisting of numerous mechanical and intellectual organs," which transforms the means of labor as a function of its *use value* into an existence suitable for *capital in general*.[5] "In the machine . . . use-value . . . is transformed into an existence adequate to fixed capital and to capital as such; and the form in which it was adopted into the production process of capital, the direct means of labor, is superseded by a form posited by capital itself and corresponding to it."[6] Machinery no longer comes between the worker and the object; on the contrary, the worker's activity is no longer engaged in making use of the instrument but, rather, in engaging with the instrument. It is the machinery that possesses the skill and strength, for it is a "virtuoso" endowed with a soul represented by the laws that operate within it. The science that forces the components of the machine to act automatically toward an end does not exist in the consciousness of the worker; now exploitation (the appropriation of objectivized living labor by capital) is embodied in automated production as an element of the production process itself. This process appears directly and immediately as a power that dominates labor; that incorporates it in the development of capital. This "supreme negation" of necessary labor is the necessary tendency of capital, realized by the automated device (a process throughout which living workers are no more than dispersed points). Additionally, the enormous production made possible eliminates from the product any relationship to the immediate needs of production, therefore, to *immediate use-value.* The accumulation of knowledge and skill, "of the general productive forces of the social brain," appears as an *attribute of capital.*[7]

Never has Marx's ability to theorize been as strong as it is here. Such, in fact, that its scope didn't become apparent until a century later, when his predictions were realized before our eyes—not without surprises and new problems.

If we refer to the texts of *The German Ideology* cited above, assuming them to remain relevant, we can form an image of Marx's idea of total revolution. Total revolution cannot be correctly defined in terms of ethics or aesthetics. Automated devices, capable of tremendous productivity, replace what was once scarcity with abundance, regardless of the population and its needs and desires. Communities, now freed of all the past limitations on communal ways of life, control those productive forces (thereby restoring them to *use*). And this takes place in an urban context, which is itself freed from the limitations inherent in what was once "the town." Members of this communist society, or the communal groups of which it is constituted, find themselves freed of any of the obligations and constraints imposed by what was once labor. They are dedicated to nonlabor. The activities in which they engage, and especially the intellectual (scientific) activities through which they form the "social brain" that dominates its material organs (automated devices), cannot be compared with work. Most important, neither activity per se nor its results can be measured in units of time. Nonwork has replaced work.

Are we not immersed in a world of science fiction? Utopia? How do we reach this supreme stage? How can we control these devices and colossal productive forces, simultaneously generated and monopolized by capitalism, when those devices incorporate the labor force while dispersing the working class? Where is the battleground? Are political changes alone sufficient for this prodigious subversion, this turning of the world upside down, where the means becomes the end because the end no longer has any means?

It is not without irony that the meaning of a philosophical vocabulary has been shifted and transferred to other objectives by referring to the Marxist conception of revolutionary time as the "reign of ends."[8] This time consists of a schedule of ends: religion, philosophy, ideology, the state, politics, and so on. To this impressive list we can add the end of work and the end of the city. Work does not culminate in leisure but in nonwork. The city doesn't culminate in the countryside but in the simultaneous surpassing of city and country. This leaves a void that can be filled by the imagination, projections, and theoretical forecasts. But what do nonwork and the noncity consist of? To answer the question, we must take a step backward, toward creative activities (art) and toward the concepts that analysis has identified in the "urban," such as meetings, gatherings, the center, decentering, and so on. But one can always respond that the surpassing of work and the city will have nothing in common with what was formerly known by those terms. So, is it utopian, is it science fiction? Perhaps, but this devil of a man known as Karl Marx still has a few surprises in store for us. He's waiting. There is nothing more positive than this concept of automation. It moves forward. It "surrounds" us, as is said, by hiding beneath the natural environment and its end (only one among many, but one that is also "realized"). So, where is this utopia? At the heart of the real that it haunts. And where is "reality"? In the possible, yes, certainly. But what is possible and what is impossible?

What happens when the automated devices invade our streets, our monuments, our homes? When the combination of mechanical and intellectual elements invades the intellect itself and, in so doing, also subordinates "mankind"? When their power is such that having absorbed the workers and incorporated the "working class," which ceases to exist as such, they also absorb the user, now powerless to restore or proclaim "use value"? To these ends must we now add that of "exchange value"? How can we control the new monster, the Leviathan, the Golem? Must we accept it, attempt a compromise rather than confronting it head-on?

The supreme conflict, if we are to follow Marx, would appear at the intersection of political economy and civil society.

3

Critique of Political Economy

There was, there is a direction to Marxist thought. For Marx, it was a path laboriously cleared through a series of obstacles. Little by little, this now celebrated process was transformed into a broad avenue, then a tourist highway. It has been traversed on foot, on horseback, by automobile, and is now part of the itinerary of travel agencies. Along the highway there are well-equipped junctions, motels, and places thought best to avoid. And yet—a surprise to some—there are still sources of wonder, almost of discovery, not along the highway of the Sun, but in the landscape, the "environment," and over the horizon.

How long did it take to realize that the subtitle of *Capital*, "A Critique of Political Economy," should be taken *literally*? In spite of this, for more than half a century, *Capital* was considered to be an economic treatise. It was then interpreted as a critique of *bourgeois* political economy, containing the premises of a "socialist" political economy. However, it should be read as a critique of *all political economy*: of the economic as something "separate," of the fragmented science that is transformed into restrictive mechanisms, of the "discipline" that establishes and congeals certain momentary relationships by elevating them to the rank of so-called scientific "truths." Likewise, the Marxist critique of the state is not limited to the Hegelian state, the bourgeois state, but extends to democracy, to the so-called democratic and socialist state—of every state (as a source of power).

Between 1848 and 1867, a period of almost twenty years, Marx prepared his great work, *Capital*. But he did more than limit himself to gathering materials, citations, and figures. For there were theoretical difficulties, and initially, the problem of method. Following his polemic with Proudhon and his Hegelianism, Marx was suspicious of dialectics, returning to it only ten years later. As for his principal theoretical argument, the concept and theory of surplus value, he approached it slowly. Finally, and most importantly, I believe he miscalculated in approaching political economy, that is, the study of so-called economic reality together with its political implications, and positioned himself poorly with respect to it.

Fortunately, the Marxist problematic throughout this lengthy, but decisive, period is much clearer to us today than it was to Marx himself when he first revealed the path.

We can now retrace that path, for there are several recent publications we can examine directly.[1] We also benefit from a certain distance from the many examinations, commentaries, interpretations, and readings available, both literal and symptomatic. These successive opposed, convergent, and divergent readings have afforded us a strange theoretical experience. By unearthing this scholastic lode, we obtain a degree of freedom that enables new discoveries to be made.

I've tried to show that, for Marx, the dissolution of the feudal mode of production and the transition to capitalism was attributed to and associated with a *subject*: the city. The city shattered (simultaneously superseding itself) the medieval (feudal) system by promoting the transition to capitalist *relations of production* (of whose emergence there can be no doubt), thereby entering into a different *mode of production*—capitalism. With the emergence of the city, everything became clear for a long period of time. There was no need to choose between Subject and System because the city is a "subject" and a coherent force, a partial system that attacks the overall system, that simultaneously reveals and destroys it. But this is where Subject and System fail. If there is a system, when does it come into being? At what moment can we assert, relying on these new relations of production, that this is capitalism, clearly and distinctly systematized? Moreover, *who* is acting? What is the nature of the social *support,* the vehicle, which is initially the agent of transition and, then, serves to constitute or institute the system?

The Introduction to *A Contribution to a Critique of Political Economy* (1857) exposes Marx's hesitation. We could say that the problem of the subject represents no more than a surviving remnant of classical philosophy, an ancient language Marx's thought makes use of to find a new language. This is not completely false, as shown by the interjection of questions concerning "subject" and "object" in a series of comments on language in the Introduction. But this is not the only reason. The question of the subject is already associated with that of *production.* "Production in general is an abstraction but a rational abstraction in so far as it really brings out and fixes the common elements and thus saves us repetition."[2] It is necessary to distinguish "just those things which determine their development, i.e., the elements which are not general and common, must be separated out from the determination valid for production as such, so that in their unity—which arises already from the identity of the subject, humanity, and of the object, nature—their essential difference is not forgotten" (85). The question of subject and object is, therefore, connected to that of the specificity of the relations and modes of production. "Lastly, production also is not only a particular production. Rather, it is always a certain social body, a social subject" (86). But by remaining at this level of abstraction rather than studying *productivity* and the levels attained, concretely and practically, through an analysis of production, we end up with a tautology: wealth in general is created from objective and subjective elements. So, we eliminate differences by formulating "general human laws" (87). The temptation is great, especially for the philosopher, using philosophical language, to take "mankind" as the subject. This error was avoided when it became necessary to rely on a concrete, practical, and historical existence as substrate and agent: the city.

A difficulty also arises because there are relationships, levels, forms, and functions that, taken together, must constitute and necessarily constitute a whole. In particular, production and consumption, needs and the means to satisfy them, necessarily form a whole endowed with a certain coherence or cohesiveness. We then move, or rather leap, from *subject* to *system*. This does nothing to resolve the difficulties, however. Should we then use "society" rather than "mankind" as the subject? This is the wrong approach, for it is still philosophical and speculative, and sidesteps relations of production and the way in which production "objectively and subjectively creates" consumption and the consumer, needs and the objects that satisfy them, exchanges and the things exchanged. And if we consider the *system*, to whom can we attribute it? How can we theoretically, and practically, address its cohesion? Who or what guides the interaction of factors within the organic whole? There is no one to criticize. In opposition to the subject, too personal, we have the system, which is impersonal. If the subject ensures the imputation, the presence of a consciousness, thought, and, therefore, responsibility (more or less limited by the absence of theoretical knowledge), the system provides coherence, rationality, totality. In this way, we soon arrive at a tautology (for example, by showing the internal connection between production and consumption) and similar associations (for example, by comparing societies, historical periods), both of which erase any differences that might exist. If we must choose, how do we go about it? Shouldn't we seek another path by avoiding the dilemma of subject or system?

What about history, to which we might turn (as Marx did himself) in order to sidestep the dilemma and resolve the contradictions? Probably not. For we already know that "history" can be taken as a "subject" only if we personalize it in the manner of the theologians (Providence) or metaphysicians (Spirit, Idea). It would be difficult to make of it a system; we would have to presuppose a truth or inherent logic, once again, either theological or metaphysical.

In the case of production and consumption and their relationship, the question would present itself as follows: "Who produces and for whom?" Or, expressed differently: "What does it mean to produce? How and why produce? How and why produce more?" We know that the concept of production can be understood in two ways. There is nothing surprising in this. If a concept or a reality grasped in thought had only one meaning, did not have two different senses, contained no opposition, we would be forced to use the deductive method. All our problems would be solved, virtually, and, as in mathematics, we could even assume them to be solved and seek a solution. In the field that Marx is exploring, this is not the case. Of the two meanings of the term "production," we know that one is narrow and precise, the other broad and vague. Let us—as Marx did for years—linger over this opposition.

The twofold understanding of the term arises from the fact that "men" in society produce both things (products) and works (everything else). Things can be numbered, counted, given a monetary value, exchanged. But what about works? To produce in the broad sense is to produce science, art, interpersonal relations, time and space, events, history, institutions, society itself, the city, the state—in a word, everything. In the narrow sense, common sense comes to the fore and everyone knows what they are talking about; but thought in this area of inquiry, like practice, becomes a platitude. So, how and where do we stop? At some point, the philosopher collects himself and gathers what he has lost by saying: "Yes, mankind as a whole produces Truth, the Idea, Divinity!"

The alternative corresponds to that of subject and system but does not coincide with it. Where and how can we identify attribution? Or coherence? The production of products is impersonal; the production of works cannot be understood if it does not depend on subjects.

The economist, guilelessly, that is, with a certainty that is indistinguishable from the triviality of common sense and takes itself to be scientific truth, assumes the narrow meaning. He establishes. He counts. He describes. He can just as easily count eggs as tons of steel, cattle as well as workers. During these operations, he maintains a tranquil and unshakable certitude. The "who" and "why" don't interest him. Economic empiricism rejects concepts, theories, criticism. Does it possess understanding? Marx doesn't think so, for it has no understanding of *relationships*. Yet, when thought attempts to grasp *social relationships*, doesn't it risk losing sight of the facts? It steps back and withdraws; critical appreciation finds its place, but isn't it criticism itself (of "real" society, of the empiricism that is satisfied with facts) that motivates the conceptualization of relationships?

In the Introduction—no one who is familiar with his thought is unaware of it—Marx settles the fate of history. For a long time he believed that this knowledge, the highest form of knowledge, the most vast, would enable him to understand modern society by illustrating its formation. He still believed this in 1845 when he wrote *The German Ideology* with Engels, even though the first signs of doubt had begun to emerge. Wasn't this confidence in history still a form of Hegelianism? With respect to antiquity and the Middle Ages, history as a science of becoming was still fairly reliable. Thought discovered both the "subject" and the cohesion of the subject as "agent." But what about the modern era? In truth, when theory comprises antiquity and the Middle Ages, it already makes use of the modern era and its categories, their presence and absence in previous eras. "Bourgeois society is the most developed and the most complex historic organization of production. The categories which express its relations, the comprehension of its structure, thereby also allow insights into the structure and the relations of production of all the vanished social formations out of whose ruins and elements it built itself up, whose partly still unconquered remnants are carried along within it, whose mere nuances have developed explicit significance within it, etc." (105). These categories can also contain them in a developed or degraded form, or as caricature, in such a way that *difference* remains essential; the result being that we cannot invoke historical evolution to critically understand and appreciate the current form of society, bourgeois society. Even the invocation of the past creates a mythology. The opposite approach is needed. We must start from the present, from its "categories," its critical comprehension, to understand the past, feudalism, antiquity. History cannot replace political economy and the critique of political economy!

What, then, is the legitimate theoretical approach? "In the succession of the economic categories, as in any other historical, social science, it must not be forgotten that their subject—here, modern bourgeois society—is always what is given, in the head as well as in reality, and that these categories therefore express the forms of being, the characteristics of existence, and often only individual sides of this specific society, this subject, and that therefore this society by no means begins only at the point where one can speak of it *as such*; this holds *for science as well*. This is to be kept in mind because it will shortly be decisive for the order and sequence of the categories" (106). Therefore, we will not attempt to determine the evolution of bourgeois society from earlier categories (of which the city is one). We must first study industry, not agriculture. For, "in all forms of society there is one specific kind of production which predominates over the rest, whose relations thus assign rank and influence to the others" (106–7). We thus find just how much bourgeois society differs from societies in which landed property dominates, where the relationship with nature is predominant. Where capital dominates, the predominance shifts to the new social element. "Ground rent cannot be understood without capital. But capital can certainly be understood without ground rent" (107), precisely because it is there, actual, although created over the course of history. It is economic force that dominates social relationships in bourgeois society. It is, therefore, "the starting point as well as the finishing point" (ibid.). In this way, we can understand earlier societies, for example, those in which a nascent industry in the urban context imitates the organization and relationships common to the countryside, as in the Middle Ages.

Therefore, it was impossible for Marx, in 1857, to accept, as

he had ten years earlier, the town and the countryside as auton-
omous concepts and categories, handed down by history and capable of giving rise to historical time as something theoretically
intelligible. These categories are subordinate to more general categories, arising from features common to every society (production, consumption, and their internal connection, their unity) as
well as from features specific to modern society. Thus, and only
thus, do the differences come into view, methodically and theoretically developed.

Nonetheless, town and country remained essential categories in the outline Marx presented (in 1857) of the future work.
"The order obviously has to be (1) the general, abstract determi-
nants which obtain in more or less all forms of society . . . (2)
The categories which make up the inner structure of bourgeois
society and on which the fundamental classes rest. Capital, wage
labor, landed property. Their interrelation. Town and country. . . .
(3) Concentration of bourgeois society in the form of the state.
Viewed in relation to itself. The 'unproductive' classes. Taxes.
State debt. Public credit. The population. The colonies. Emigration. (4) The international relations of production. International
division of labor. . . . (5) The world market and crises" (108).

We now know that Marx would not follow his plan exactly.
Why? It is clear to us that several methodological and theoretical
problems had yet to be resolved. In particular, Marx took (bourgeois) society to be a subject, without ever asking himself what a
society or subject might be, without asking whether the bourgeoisie as a class is a *subject* coinciding with bourgeois society. From
subject he jumps to *system,* considering capital and capitalism as
one.

Looked at in this way, the other fragments of the same period
take on their full meaning. The celebrated fragment on art cannot be taken in isolation. It answers the question, "What does
it mean to produce in the broad sense?" It also responds to the
question, "What is a society?" To produce does not only imply
material production, it comprises the production of law, family

structure, a legal system, art, and so on, although not without disparities between these sectors of production. A society implies practical social relationships, of which "culture" is a part. A society cannot be reduced to production as understood by economists: an apparatus of production and consumption, identity or difference between the two aspects. To produce, for a society, is to also produce events, history, and, consequently, wars. And "war is waged before peace." Economic relationships as important as wage labor and mechanization "develop earlier, owing to war and in the armies, etc., than in the interior of bourgeois society" (109). Moreover, "the relation of productive force and relations of exchange are also especially vivid in the army" (ibid.).

The existence alone of this fragment, of extreme density and equally extreme obscurity, would suffice to show that Marx's thought, as it progressed along a path filled with obstacles, found its direction but had not yet made use of the materials at its disposal or even discovered where it was ultimately going. Paradoxical results ensued.

The draft of 1857–59, published years later, gives the impression of a certain fecund disorder, but one that is stimulating for the modern reader who comes to this after having read it in its final form in *Capital*. In the *Grundrisse*, we encounter thought working its way through its elements and problems. One preoccupation is dominant, one that never disappeared but was subsequently attenuated: an emphasis on *differences*, the need to shine a light on them, to express them in language and concepts. But economists as well as philosophers and historians forget the *specifics*. Ideologies create abstractions of specific conditions, those associated with the *determinate form* of a given production in a society, ours. If we emphasize only the content, which turns the accumulated work of the past into the necessary element of all actual work, "nothing is easier than to demonstrate that capital is a necessary condition for all human production" (258). If this is a proof, it is a fallacious one because this homogenizing thought ignores *specific conditions*. In the *Grundrisse* everything is perceived and conceived in terms of *difference*, and this includes Asiatic societies and the Asiatic "mode of production" in contrast to Western societies and their development.

A second paradox arises because, when viewed in terms of the actual, history, the past, and its evolution can be seen in sharp relief. Its features become sharper, do not blur in the distance or lose themselves in the historical past. This is especially true of the city and the "town–country" relationship. What was said by Marx in earlier works reappears here with renewed vigor.

Concerning the city, there was no "urban mode of production" any more than a "landed" or "agrarian mode of production." Likewise, for Marx, there is no "industrial society" any more than there is an "industrial revolution." And yet, the land, the countryside, the town, industry all play an essential role in the becoming of human society, in the transformation of production, relations and modes of production.

Land is the material support of societies. But it is hardly unchangeable. Its appearance changes from pure, primal nature to ravaged landscape. As a support of human societies, from the origin to the end of mankind, it is neither immutable nor passive. The land is first and foremost "the great laboratory" that supplies the instrument and working material of labor, as well as where it takes place (cf. *Capital*, volume 1, part 3, chapter 8, on land and its relation to labor, a passage that incorporates and expands some of the ideas found in the *Grundrisse*). Men, in association with one another, constituting a society, dominate nature, modify the earth and its elements, remove the means necessary for their activity, distance themselves from nature, and substitute another reality, their own, even one that is factitious. The earth is no longer the initial laboratory. But what will replace it? The city. The changing relationship between town and country (and the word *changing* signifies "conflictual") is the permanent foundation of social change. What, then, is the city? Like the land on which it rests, it is a *medium*, an *intermediary*, a *mediation*, a *means*, the most extensive, most important of all. The transformation of nature and the earth implies another site, another milieu: the city. Although there is no "urban mode of production" any more than there is an "agrarian mode of production," the city, or more precisely its relationship to the countryside, implements changes in production by serving as both *receptacle* and *condition,* site and milieu. In and around the city, nature yields to a second nature. In this way, the city traverses the modes of production, processes that begin once the urban commune replaces the community (tribal or agrarian), which is closely tied to the land. The city rather than the land becomes the great laboratory of social forces.

In general, the commune arises from the community (tribe or village) as its preexisting condition. The transition from the community, where nature predominates, along with its immediate connections (blood, family, location, and natural features), to the urban commune implies considerable changes in ownership, production, and exchange. During the course of these modifications, "social nature" is substituted for immediate nature. While nature as such appears to the individual in the primitive community as both resource and enemy, ally and deadly threat, social nature treats the member of society as an outsider. The result of combined labor is forced upon vital activity as an external power, so that neither labor nor its product is any longer the property of the workers. Little by little, collective or combined labor appears as *objectivity* (alien ownership) and *subjectivity* (alien power) (cf. p. 470). In this way, the intrinsic power of the social being is turned against itself as an "animated monster." The city becomes the general locus of this transformation. Shouldn't it be the "animated monster," then? Possibly, although Marx doesn't say as much.

There are differences, however. In Asian societies, where the monarch retains the surplus product of agricultural labor, we see the growth of administrative cities that also serve as military camps; here, the monarch can exchange his income "against free hands." This does not constitute wage labor, even though the activity of these "free hands" can stand in opposition to slavery and serfdom (467). In this case, the countryside directly and immediately supplies the base. This countryside consists of small agrarian communities that allow for the establishment of a superior unity. "For example, it is not in the least a contradiction to it that, as in most of the Asiatic land-forms, the comprehensive unity standing above all these little communities appears as the higher proprietor or as the sole proprietor; the real communities hence only as hereditary possessors" (472–73). Because this unity is the real owner and higher condition of communal ownership, "it follows that this unity can appear as a particular entity above the many real particular communities" (473). This supreme unity, this despotic government, is situated in the oriental city.

In Asian societies, the sovereign unity of society, the Unique, which has ownership of all the land of the communities and individuals, has the city as its seat and resource. The oriental city is established alongside villages, which the despotic state administers while exploiting them, either at locations where external commerce can take place or "where the head of the state and his satraps exchange their revenue (surplus product) for labor, spend it as labor-fund" (474). In these societies, individual property can never be sufficient; the direct link between the community and nature cannot be broken; irrigation and the control of the water supply, which are essential to the life of the community, are the responsibility of the state, which thereby assumes a direct economic role, acting on productive forces, monitoring nature, and maintaining its relationship to society.

Thus reigns the supreme Unity, the despot incarnating the common element in local peasant communities—absolute paternity. The social surplus product, determined as a function of the real appropriation of labor, that is, leaving the villagers with enough to live on, covers the general expenses of administration and large-scale construction; the remainder goes to the Unique. This enormous wealth enables him to engage in large-scale endeavors: wars, celebrations, construction projects. "Amidst oriental despotism and the propertylessness which seems legally to exist there, this clan or communal property exists in fact as the foundation, created mostly by a combination of manufactures and agriculture within the small commune, which thus becomes altogether self-sustaining, and contains all the conditions of re-production and surplus production within itself" (473). The su-preme community assumes the aspect of a transcendent *person*. Surplus labor in the form of tribute, collective labor itself, is part of the cult of the human and divine, real and imaginary, unity—the sovereign.

These texts were recently exhumed when the question of the "Asiatic mode of production" was reexamined. The concept doesn't appear in them, however; Marx only wrote about "Asiatic societies." However, the concept of the Asiatic mode of produc-tion is already present, in the sense that it designates a number of societies unlike Western societies through the arrangement and relationship of their fundamental elements: country and town, divisions of labor, state and sovereignty. We know from Marx's other texts, although widely dispersed, that he had de-veloped very precise ideas about the specific features of history in Asiatic societies. Great empires are established on the basis of agrarian communities; they endure through inertia; they collapse under the blows of conquerors but reconstitute themselves in a way that is analogous to what they were before their fall. History has a repetitive nature owing to the stability, or rather the stagna-tion, of productive forces, which is to say, agrarian communities and their organization. As for the cities, whose role is decisive as the seat of despotic sovereignty, they do not escape the caprices of despots. Sometimes they share the stability of the economic-social-political whole, when their site is particularly favorable; sometimes they disappear with an empire and are reconstructed elsewhere, as centers of administrative and military action.[3] In the *Grundrisse*, Marx implies that these ideas or hypotheses do not only apply to the various Asiatic societies but, possibly, to pre-Columbian America, Mexico, Peru, and so on (ibid.). Through labor, the unity can extend to the entire community, organized as a formal system, not only on the local communal scale but for all of society.

The concept of an Asiatic mode of production is built upon these analyses, which Marx had always wanted to return to as they highlight a fundamental theme of his: the interrelation of forms of ownership in correlation with the relationship between town and country. The concept was never developed into a theory, at least not by Marx. What about recent efforts, undertaken since the publication of [Karl A.] Wittfogel's well-known work on oriental despotism? Have they provided us with a theory? Such a theory would only assume its full depth and breadth if the functions of the oriental city—multiple (religious, military, political, administrative, economic) and specific functions—together with an organization centralized in time and space, are fully examined. Marx began to elaborate such a theory but was far from completing it. If the concept obscures the differences not only within Asiatic societies but in European societies as well, if it's no more than a simple means of classifying facts by arranging them into general and homogeneous categories, so-called Marxist theory would once again lag behind Marx's written works.

What was Marx trying to say by calling the earth a "laboratory"? The soil is a force. The productive forces comprise labor—means of production, instruments and machines—scientific techniques and understanding—nature and its resources. Certain "purists" will protest, insisting that this order be reversed; their dogmatism is such that they suspect the presence of a political intention in an enumeration that fails to place *workers* in the final and supreme rank, historically and scientifically. But let us move on from this scholastic hairsplitting. Marx's use of the word *laboratory* means that nature does not remain a passive element of production. It intervenes, for the simple reason that humans in a group (forming a society and "producing" their social existence) struggle with it. Production, as an act occurring between man and nature, allows nature to reply to human initiatives. It is not satisfied with supplying materials that productive activity removes, isolates, and transforms. The community comes from nature as a community of blood, customs, and language. This first *condition* of the social appropriation of *objective conditions,* the community, arises from nature in very different ways, nature itself being extraordinarily diverse. It seems that, for Marx, the organizational structures of "primitive" communities were highly varied but selected by the struggle against primal nature. Some disappeared, others faded away, others became fossilized. Few experienced the prosperity or development that resulted in civilization, that is, the city. The city, in turn, by substituting itself for "objective" nature as a condition of appropriation, took precedence as a laboratory. Among the cities and urban agglomerations, some faded away and disappeared, others barely survived; still others grew stagnant. Few underwent the process of growth and development that led to the growth of productive forces and created higher social formations. Like the earth, the city represents a productive force (but not a means of production, an instrument). By providing an opportunity for the coming together of workers and work, knowledge, and technologies, and the means of production themselves, it played an active role in growth and development. It can, therefore, also counteract them. The confrontation within it, on its territory, of productive forces and relations of production can have effects that are either beneficial or disastrous. Like the earth, like the nation, in confronting them, the city becomes, over the course of history, the crucible in which relations of production are developed, in which the conflicts between relations of production and productive forces are brought out into the open.

The European West, in comparison with Asiatic societies, also reveals a second form of transformation of the agrarian community. This "second form . . . like the first . . . has essential modifications brought about locally, historically, etc." (474). The fruit of a life and historical destiny that are more tumultuous than in Asia, it assumes a *community,* but the tribal basis of that community has been transformed by nomadism, by migration—the first detachment of the social being from nature. Unlike the Asian form, the European form does not preserve the natural community as substance and content. This gives the urban form a reality unlike that of the Asiatic city. This society does not have the countryside and nature "in itself" as its basis, but the city, erected as a seat (center) for those who live in the countryside, the owners of the land. The fields already represent the territory of the city rather than the village. Thus, the city will be Athens or Rome but not Samarkand or Peking. In the West, nature and the earth do not require such immense collective labor (irrigation, dams, drainage) and do not present, "in themselves," obstacles to those who wish to work and appropriate them. Western societies, which already have instability, nomadism, and migration as their initial condition, are therefore condemned to aggression. "War is therefore the great comprehensive task, the great communal labor" (ibid.) required either to take possession of the land from the existing communities who occupy it or to maintain its occupation against aggressors. Nature is maintained within this society as a permanent struggle for life. Society is first organized militarily rather than administratively as in the East. Wars are selective; they take place between cities. *The city is the basis of this military organization.* Within the urban context, tribal connections are maintained but are also transformed. Private property is separated from communal property when the urban commune grows into a state.

In this form of association, individual property has ceased to coincide with *immediate* communal property because the bond with nature has been severed. The commune relies on landowners who are still workers (peasants) at the outset and only later landed property owners who no longer work. The urban commune, under the form of the state, consists in a reciprocal relationship with these "private," although free and equal, owners; it protects and supports them. The *ager publicus* provides collective needs. The product of a history, both as reality and as consciousness, this urban commune remains the condition of all (public and private) ownership of the land, but for the individual member of the commune "this belonging [is] mediated by his being a member of the state, by the being of the state—hence by a presupposition regarded as divine" (475). The analogies between the ancient polis and the oriental city, that is, certain religious, military, and political features, are unable to conceal the differences. The oriental city does not escape the "immediacy" of the bond with nature that will influence and even fashion its institutions and ideas, whereas the ancient polis has lost that immediacy and acquired the characteristic of *mediation* that will mark its destiny.

The city harbors a great concentration of wealth and people, and its territory incorporates the surrounding countryside. Wealth grows through productive labor: small agriculture, artisans, and small manufacturing (spinning, weaving, forges and small metallurgical operations, ceramics). But it is mostly through warfare that the urban community grows in size and wealth. However, for a long time, "the individual is placed in such conditions of earning his living as to make not the acquiring of wealth his object, but self-sustenance, his own reproduction as a member of the community" (476). This was a time when the ancient urban republics thrived. Excess time and the social surplus product returned to the urban commune and, consequently, contributed to a communal effort: warfare. During these bellicose struggles, which were incessant and terrible, and which characterized Greek and Roman civilization, some cities, those better equipped and better organized for war, the "successful" cities, like Athens and Rome, prospered.

We can now risk a remark that is not without theoretical importance. In the pages of the *Grundrisse* discussed so far, Marx has studied the formation of the city of antiquity. He considers it to be a "second form" of historicity, of historical destiny or development, the first form being the oriental city in Asiatic societies. He characterizes the antique city by a few essential traits, primarily its character of *mediation,* which had broken with *immediacy* (the direct connection with nature, still prevalent in the

Asiatic community, as in the earliest consanguineal or familial tribal communities) but was not completely divorced from the immediate, from the earth, nature, and agriculture. Marx does not even allude to *slaves*. But this does not mean he has neglected this important fact. Several texts illustrate this, especially those in which he illustrates the differences between slaves and modern workers. With respect to the city of antiquity, its genesis and formal makeup, he illustrates the *conditions of slavery*. Slaves appear as an additional mediation between the citizen and the land, between the free member of the urban community and the productive labor that provides him with a greater degree of responsibility, initially for politics and warfare, and then for personal gain. This will lead the city to its glory or its ruin.[4] Money and the thirst for money will undermine these ancient communities. The city, not yet completely freed from the countryside, had to see itself broken and corrupted by money before being liberated from that connection. In Rome and Greece, money first appeared innocently enough in a form reflected in its two primary functions: as a reference standard and as a means of circulation. But with the development of trade or, in the case of Rome, when conquest brought with it rivers of money, suddenly, at a given level of economic development, money appeared necessarily in its third function, "and the further it develops in that role, the more the decay of their community advances" (223). The third function of money is its generalized purchasing power, which turns money into capital.

We may very well ask if the concept of a "slave mode of production" does not emphasize a belated and destructive aspect of the ancient city. This aspect assumes its full importance and value only in the confrontation with capitalism; in itself, in terms of the genealogy of the ancient city out of the community of blood, it is a derived trait. It has little importance alongside the essential relationship between town and country, that is, society and nature, historical and original, and so on. It condenses becoming, summarizes the apogee and waning away of the ancient city. In this sense, we can preserve the concept by limiting it, by relativizing and subordinating it to essential relationships.

In the *Grundrisse,* the ancient city appears as a *second* line of development followed by decline, the *first* line being the oriental city. There is a *third* form, a third line of development in the West, namely, the one that grows out of the barbarian Germanic communities (474–79). Although minimal in appearance, there is a difference among these forms. In the East, possession remains with the community, even that of the Unique, the Sovereign. In the city of antiquity, two distinct forms of ownership are present, which are united in the urban context: private property, that of the citizen, and public property, that of the polis, the *ager publicus.* In the Germanic tribal community, three forms of ownership are found: private property (a house, a portion of the arable land); collective property, which depends on the group of owners and not on the village or town as such; and, finally, shared ownership, communal land or the land of the people, which was quite distinct from individual properties and their shared ownership. These include lands for hunting and pasturing, forests, and so on (483).

This is a radical difference, for it means that the city in the European West (Germany, France, England, Spain) is not an entity greater than its members but an association. And it is this that determined its historical future.

To sum up, Marx identifies three lines of development that followed the dissolution of the consanguineal community, the appearance of communitarian and communal forms of territorial occupation (use and then exchange), the formation of the "town–country" relationship, and its transformation. A first line leads society and the city to stagnation. A second leads both the city and society to rapid growth and unparalleled prestige, followed by decline. A third orientation leads the city, in its relationship to the country, to slow growth but a future without identifiable limits. The first form is unitary, the second binary, and the last tripartite.[5]

For Marx, in 1857, the question preoccupied him to such an

extent that he focused at great length on the differences mentioned above. It's possible, in the absence of conclusive historical documents and his reliance on several incomplete works (Niebuhr and others), that he experienced difficulty in developing his ideas with sufficient clarity, so his discussion here retains an element of hypothesis, a philosophy of history.

Although Asian history reveals "a series of undifferentiated units of town and country," although the history of classical antiquity consists of a history of the city as a center of rural life, having as its basis landed property and agriculture, the Middle Ages begins in the countryside, the historical center, and develops through the violent opposition between town and country. "The modern [age] is the urbanization of the countryside, not ruralization of the city as in antiquity" (479). This is a decisive formula that illustrates the essential dialectical movement. Development has not yet reached its fullest expression, it has covered the field of the possible only where the contradictory aspect of the town–country relationship was found, where the conflict reached its extreme manifestation. This conflict did not exist in the Orient. So the splendor, the grandeur, the power of the oriental cities of high antiquity, from the time of Babylon, Susa, or Nineveh, until today, was in vain. Splendor and power are not enough. Cities follow one another, replace one another, grow and die like empires. In the city of antiquity, those who lost the battle won the war (or, if you prefer, those who won the battle lost the war). Superficially successful at the outset, its subsequent loss is irreversible—in spite of the glory of Athens and Rome and their conquests. Dominating the countryside politically, it was then dominated by it economically. This conflict, which did not progress to its ultimate conclusion, led to the breakdown of the city. Here, too, beauty and splendor were unable to prevent destiny from unfolding. Rather, it carried out the decree of the so-called historical powers. As for the humble merchant cities of the European West, not only did they have their own history, they made history. They were indeed the "subject." This played out during a life-and-death struggle that was already a form of class struggle, and because they were based on an associative model (the oath being only one aspect of this principle of association).

The Western city, through a historical destiny that had nothing to do with theological predestination, would become the site and context of an extraordinary reversal: dominant nature will in turn be dominated. This is not to say that the city, the site of antiphysis, by this fact alone is a power favorable to mankind, a second mother welcoming those who fled the first, who have succeeded in cutting the umbilical cord. But let's not get ahead of ourselves, or Marx.

The original barbarian commune (Germanic) does not coincide with the city. It acquires neither an existence greater than that of its members nor an independent economic and political existence. "Among the Germanic tribes, where the individual family chiefs settled in the forests, long distances apart, the commune exists, already from outward observation, only in the periodic gathering-together *[Vereinigung]* of the commune members, although their *unity-in-itself* is posited in their ancestry, language, common past and history, etc." (483). The commune, under these conditions, does not become, in the form of a city, a "state system"; it cannot become, through its various functionaries, an entity outside its general assemblies. Ownership by the individual and the family group is not mediated by the commune; on the contrary, it's the existence of the commune and its holdings that is mediated by the relationships among its members. The economic totality is contained in every home, in every family. Whereas the ancient city, "with its rural market, forms an economic totality," the landowner is also a citizen (urban), and citizenship can be summarized in one simple figure alone: the peasant, inhabitant of the city.

For the barbarians, the commune didn't present itself as a substance in which the individual would be an accident. It is neither a unity created through the existence of the city and its needs nor a unity occurring in the urban territory. It is not suddenly separated from the community of language and blood, the production of use values, or relationships in which the reproduction of individuals is implied. Proprietors lose these relationships very slowly, that is, "the relation of the working (producing or self-reproducing) subject to the conditions of his production or reproduction as his own" (495).

This loss of the bipartite relationship that makes the individual both a citizen equal to other members of the commune and an owner is inevitable, especially when the village becomes a town following the growth of productivity. In the West, with the foundation of barbarian communities, this loss was minimized. But in the East, it was never carried to fruition, it was blocked; and in the ancient city, it "dissolves the mode of production on which the community rests, and, with it, the objective individual, i.e. the individual defined as Roman, Greek, etc." (ibid.). The social unit assumes a specific communal form and the ownership of nature associated with it assumes a living reality in a specific *mode of production* (emphasis is Marx's) that consists in a relationship among individuals as well as the relationship between their totality and nature, which entails a specific mode of labor (family activity and communal labor). In this way, the community itself represents the first great productive force and, depending on the type of production (stock breeding, agriculture), we see the development of a particular mode of production and particular forces of production, both objective and subjective (ibid.).

The dissolution of these relationships, the loss of support to the individual they brought about being inevitable, we now know how and why the conditions of the transition to a higher level of productivity were so much better in the West. It is here rather than in the ancient world or the East that the "animal of the flock"—rural or urban—becomes the *political animal*. Because exchange was an essential agent of this process, "it makes the herd superfluous and dissolves it." But this dissolution was disastrous in the majority of cases. The lesser evil? The member of the commune, having lost his land, and nature, and his immediate connection to them, as well as his share in a community that had made him a "proprietor," as a worker retains ownership of his instrument of labor. This occurs in a particular form of manufacturing—artisanal labor. Labor is both artistic and an end in itself; skill ensures the possession of the proper instruments. The mode of labor is transmitted through inheritance, together with the instrument and the organization of work. This is how the "medieval system of cities" functioned (497).

We know that this urban system had extensive associations, "the system of guilds and guild-masters" being one part of it. It assumes that the worker can support himself until he has completed his work. This worker possesses a "consumption fund," either through inheritance or gain, or as co-owner in a community, the guild, which sets this use aside for him on the basis of its laws and traditions (498). This assumes that such necessity is not imposed upon the worker as an external power, that of capital, because the worker, as a living force, is an immediate element of the objective conditions of production. Subservient, no doubt, but he is still not separated from his own labor, whereas under capitalism, "the worker is not a condition of production, only work is" (ibid.).

Capital implies a relation of nonownership (negative relation) to raw materials, instruments, and means of subsistence. Above all, it implies *nonownership of the land*, the negation of the conditions that derive from nature and the immediate relations between work, the elements of work, and the worker himself, the "working subject." This dissolution takes place in several stages. During the first stage, the proprietor works the land he possesses; this condition prevails in the village, among barbarian communities. The second stage is characterized by the artisanal proprietor in the urban commune. This second historical level exists side by side or outside the first. The commune and the communal association become increasingly remote from primitive, immediate (natural) forms. For, "the community on which this form of property [is] founded . . . [which is] already a produced, made, derived and secondary community, produced by the worker himself," is the (medieval) urban community (499). What characterizes the guild system, based on artisanal and urban labor, is that it reduces the community to the relation between the worker and the instrument of production alone, ownership—legitimated through skill—only affecting the tool. This relation differs radically from that established by ownership of the soil.

The dissolution of this relation, that of the worker to the instrument, will produce capitalism. Isn't it "at bottom the formula of slavery and bondage, which is likewise negated, posited as a historically dissolved condition, in the relation of the worker to the conditions of production as capital" (500). Marx will not retain this very Hegelian approach to the construction of capital through negativity and synthesis. In the *Grundrisse,* this procedure introduces new considerations, for example, those associated with the city of antiquity. The dissolution of the bond between the different elements of production did not result in a proletariat in the modern sense, any more than a community of artisans, but rather plebeians, demanding bread and circuses. Likewise, although fundamentally different, the relation between the lord and his retainers was altered. In these diverse situations, the dissolution of the relations of ownership gave way to a *relation of domination.* The relation of domination and servitude thus belongs to the decay of the relation between ownership and production; at the same time, it expresses their narrowness and brings about the turmoil of transformation. Such a relation of power was prevalent in Imperial Rome, but we find it in all processes of dissolution, including the dissolution that takes place during the so-called Renaissance period—together with the typical things that accompany such dissolution: clients, imaginary or real services, rivalries, and wars. "It will be seen on closer inspection that all these processes of dissolution mean the dissolution of relations of production in which: use value predominates" (502). This is an irony of history. Whatever remains of "use value" in the ancient or medieval cities must disappear; this disappearance will give rise to a very particular kind of "value," to very old customs: the violent exercise of wealth and power. And it is through this process that the domination of exchange clears a path forward. In relations of power, the provision of goods and services in kind takes precedence over payments. Money, that animated monster among monsters, together with that other monster, the state, attempts to impose peace, its own peace, a deadly peace: that of the world of merchandise (see ibid.). Things change, however, but they do so by their bad side!

This genesis of monetary wealth and money assumes that a dam has broken—the dam of the medieval guilds. In the system of urban guilds, ordinary money can be used for very little; only guild money, master's money, can be used to purchase looms. Money becomes the master of these masters only when it has succeeded in stripping guild workers of the means (subsistence, materials, tools) they formerly had in their possession. As for labor, whether qualified or not, capital soon finds it already available, "partly as a result of the urban guild system, partly as a result of domestic industry, or industry which is attached to agriculture as an accessory" (505). The historical process is not the result of capital but its presupposition. This history ignores the sentimental fables in which the capitalist and the worker form an association. "There is no trace [of this] in the conceptual development of capital" (ibid.). Capitalism arises from the dissolution of the urban guilds, not from any sort of participation in them. It turns out that manufacturing and the corporation coexisted, and manufacturing, already capitalist, developed in a context that arose in an earlier age. This was the situation of the Italian cities, a local phenomenon, according to Marx. Elsewhere (especially in England), the conflict assumed its full force; the new conditions, those of capitalism, increased greatly in scale, enabling it to become the dominant force.

Obviously, this history makes one conclusion obvious. By itself, the existence of monetary wealth or its supremacy (power relations) was not sufficient for the *dissolution* of ancient societies to result in capitalism. "Or else ancient Rome, Byzantium etc. would have ended their history with free labor and capital, or rather begun a new history. There, too, the dissolution of the old property relations was bound up with [the] development of monetary wealth—of trade etc. But instead of leading to industry, this dissolution led in fact to the supremacy of the countryside over the city" (506).

Thousands, millions of times, Marx's path has been reduplicated, retraced. By politicians, philosophers, economists, historians, teachers, countless students, in countries in the East, West, North, and South—a highway with travel agents and organized tours, as well as roadblocks and wrong turns.

Wouldn't every specialized reading of Marx the philosopher or Marx the economist be erroneous? The process Marx studied and which his thinking implied cannot be reduced to any specialization. The genesis or genealogy of the "urban system" (together with the guild system) in western Europe during the Middle Ages comprises a history, a political economy, a politics, but cannot be understood by separating these fields.

I have closely retraced Marx's path, namely, the genesis of the "urban system" as one step in the much larger formation of generalized exchange value, the world of commodities and money, in a word, of capital. On every occasion, the concept became more concrete as it expanded but, most important, with every new examination, *differences* appeared. The reexamination, the repetition of this trajectory has not established a tautological identity, that of truths increasingly general and vacuous. On the contrary. There were differences in the original community, immediate and natural, as numerous as languages and customs, the relations between members of the community and surrounding nature. Differences that gave rise to dissolution and arose from dissolution, that of the original community (tribal, family), that of the commune that grew up on its ruins, the ancient polis, the medieval town, different lines of evolution, some leading to stagnation, others to decline, and others opening up toward "history" and thus producing modern society, with its good and bad sides, which are inseparable. At every step of this prodigiously complex becoming, at every moment, there existed a terrifying "pressure of selection." The term is not found in Marx but corresponds to the translation of his thought into modern language: history arises dialectically from prehistory; the social being emerges from animality. A biological term evokes this transitional process quite well. Magnificent creations, splendid forms were purely and simply dissolved, destroyed, eliminated: the city of antiquity, the medieval town, among others (the oriental city followed a different temporal path than ours).

This analysis of becoming only infrequently uses general or generic entities such as "mankind" or "mode of production." I again want to emphasize this last point. The "mode of production" as a clearly determined theoretical concept and as a term denoting a society or group of societies does not appear in the *Grundrisse* either with respect to oriental societies or to ancient or medieval European societies. Nor does it appear when discussing so-called primitive communities (defined by consanguinity or territory, tribalism or family ties) other than in a highly restrictive sense. Every community has its mode of production, for it has its own language, customs, extended or local territory, its principal activity (hunting, fishing, grazing, agriculture, domestic industry, as well as highly diverse combinations of these elements), in short, an immediate relationship with nature in all its aspects— biological and animal life, resources, parental bonds, and so on.

The term "mode of production" and its conceptual associations are formulated with the rigidity and fixity we are all too familiar with in a famous passage, which has been widely commented on and which is said to condense Marxist thought: "In broad outlines we can designate the Asiatic, the ancient, the feudal and the modern bourgeois methods of production as so many epochs in the progress of the economic formation of society. The bourgeois relations of production are the last antagonistic form of the social process of production . . . The social formation constitutes, therefore, the closing chapter of the prehistory of human society."[6]

However, this text, so well known that no work on Marx and Marxism can refrain from quoting it, leads to an endless series of questions and insoluble theoretical problems if it is interpreted literally. And this is precisely what scholarly commentators have done ever since this "contribution to the critique of political economy" was inserted into—or, rather, dropped from—the Marxist vulgate.

1. How and why does the "Asiatic mode of production" become a stage in the march of progress thus identified? This is a question that has gone unanswered and has allowed (especially during the Stalinist period) Asiatic societies and their evolution and differences (among themselves and in relation to Western societies) to be obscured.

2. Assumed to be entities, that is, totalities, these "modes of production" have become so predetermined that the transition between them becomes unintelligible. The transitions disappear through enchantment or sleight of hand. Proceeding in this way, the scholarly reading of Marx disintegrates his thought. Exegesis claims to be rigorous, but it abandons literality, the only definitive yardstick, even as it manages to approach it with a narrowness that assumes itself to be the guarantor of orthodoxy. But Marx begins with a restrictive clause, "In broad outlines. . . ." What better and clearer way to say that the concept "mode of production" is *reductive,* that it retains, in every period as well as in its overall becoming, only general and uniform features? It enables us to classify periods but leaves differences aside.

3. When presented dogmatically, the concept clashes theoretically with the very clear methodological statement made by Marx: "*Dialectic of the concepts productive force (means of production) and relation of production,* a dialectic whose boundaries are to be determined, and which does not suspend the real difference."[7]

That is why, in these pages devoted to the *Grundrisse*, I have not engaged in the abstract construction of entities—"modes of production"—but in the analysis of a becoming, the formation of a dialectical process that encompasses the full extent of that becoming, based on a relation of conflict, that between town and country, which is virtually present from the start, but actualizes itself, transforms itself, engenders new forms, some of which disappear and some of which grow stronger until their emergence into history (or "prehistory," this point remains obscure).

How is capitalism established? Its domination is the result of this long process, which is both economic and political. It does not have a precise date; we cannot say, as a historian might, as if capital were a historical category, "From this moment, capitalism existed." The formation of capital and capitalism undergoes a phase involving the "formal surrender of labor to capital" (462). This, which is to say large-scale industry owned by a bourgeoisie, comes to dominate existing productive forces, forces that do not yet correspond to capitalist relations of production and the capitalist mode of production: artisans, factories, highly variable units of agricultural production and commercial exchange. The essential factor during this transformation remains immediate labor, as it is found among the trades and manufacturers, which large-scale industrial production managed to incorporate. For capitalism, these were preexisting elements, and its formation was based on their submission. In the majority of cases, political intervention accelerated and reinforced the economic process, thereby completing the extension of the market and the concentration of capital. For a long time, existing capital was still in the process of formation and the average rate of profit was not even apparent for there was no competition for capital on the market for capital, only competition on the market for products. During this period, the rate of surplus value (a relation between profit and wages) had greater importance than the rate of profit. Throughout this process, the city played a very important role in subordinating existing productive forces to capital, in serving as the site of the accumulation of capital, helping to expand markets, contributing to the formation of an average rate of profit, and, finally, providing an opportunity for political intervention. At the conclusion of the process, all that was visible was the productive force of capital rather than labor.

However, we shouldn't extrapolate from the above considerations and compare the conflict-laden mobility of social relations to this picture of fixed modes of production and established structures. In doing so we would continue to evade Marx's dialectical thought process and replace an error with its opposite illusion. The relation between town and country is a social relation, it is acquired. It entails relationships of conflict: nature versus society, immediacy versus mediation. It develops and is transformed. The theoretical concept that designates it is specific: it is a *historical category*. We might assume, following Marx, that *Weltgeschichte,* world history, arises with the city, of the city, and in the city: the oriental city, the ancient city, the medieval city. But where did this historical movement lead us? To the dawn of capitalism.

The contradiction between town and country was, for a long time (from the origins to the formation of the bourgeoisie and the predominance of commercial capital and manufacturing), a profound, a principal, an essential contradiction for a considerable number of historical societies, which is to say, societies that died in spite of their splendor. Did the principal contradiction remain during the rise of capitalism? According to Marx, it did not. It was subordinated to other contradictions, in particular those that arose from the relation of production: capital-wages, that is, to surplus value, its formation as well as its distribution and, consequently, to *class* contradictions.

The contradictory nature of the town–country relationship gradually faded away. The town overtook the countryside, society overtook unsullied nature. The original situation was reversed with the rise of the urban bourgeoisie. The town urbanized the countryside; with the waning of the Middle Ages, this significant historical outcome was finalized.

Marx wanted to show that historical becoming "advances" by its bad side. Of course, productive forces grow, social power develops an advantage over nature. But this growth has as its correlative the formation of a contrary power, which weighs on society as a whole, but especially on labor and laborers. While immense possibilities presented themselves, there was also an element of despair. In what did this power consist? How could it be described? It was referred to objectively as "capital" and subjectively as the "bourgeoisie," but from the point of view of knowledge, it had another name, which a banal ideology attempted to validate: *political economy*.

The city, to the extent that it is bound to productive forces and productive force itself, is the seat of the economic and its monstrous power. In it, during the course of history (its own), exchange value has slowly vanquished use value. This struggle was written on the walls of cities, on their buildings, in their streets; cities bear its trace, they bear witness. Likewise, the city is the seat of political power, which guarantees the economic power of capital, which protects (bourgeois) ownership of the means of production and ensures that excess and violence are prevented. The state has a variety of means available to it: the army, the police, as well as political economy and ideology (which is not additive because, for Marx, political economy is already ideological, which does not mean that it is in any way effective). The city also facilitates political struggle against political power by consolidating populations and concentrating needs, demands, and aspirations along with the means of production. In this sense, it harbors a contradiction, which cannot be eliminated and may even become more pronounced, but which can no longer be assumed to be pivotal (a driving force).

After the *Grundrisse*, it could be assumed that Marx would continue his attack, by extending and accentuating the historical vision. He could have treated history as sidestepping, deflecting, reversing the economic, with becoming deploying its irresistible power and sweeping away all obstacles. Of course, for a short period of time (between 1845 and 1848) Marx did hold this view. From this vantage point, he could have extended Hegel's concepts and held that the (French) revolution created the state and that the (proletarian) revolution would abolish that state. He could also have considered that the conflict between "society and nature" would one day rebound, experience a new fate, and reveal a surprising reversal of fortune. Certainly, Marx considered these hypotheses, various fragments show this, yet he was to abandon them. Why?

Under capitalism, political economy is essential. It is not a question of some random result of historical becoming, which this becoming would destroy the way a flood sweeps away a dam. The situation is more complex. Of course, historical societies had their economic basis; there is no society without "production" in the narrow sense of the term. Nonetheless, in societies of the past, the most important social relationships were not economic. In medieval societies, for example, hierarchical relations were constructed on an economic basis but could not be reduced to them; the relationships of violence between lords and vassals were "extra-economic" because they could be used to skim a surplus from agricultural and artisanal labor through direct pressure, which economic mechanisms (which would gradually arise but did not exist at the outset: the market, money) did not allow. In short, characterized by their primitivism and violence, which was still natural, the characteristic social relationships of medieval societies were defined for Marx as *personal* relationships, immediate and, therefore, *transparent* (see *Capital,* volume 1, part 1, chapter 4). The same was true for social relations in the town and the relations between the town and the countryside. In spite of their antagonistic character or, rather, because of that character and its immediacy, these relationships were transparent, notwithstanding the masks and vestments that identified roles, people, their place, position, and social status. These societies had an economic basis but the structures and superstructures, although unable to cut themselves free from the base, possessed a degree of freedom that has since disappeared. That is why philosophy, knowledge, law and logic, an ambiguous mix of science and ideology, and religion itself are of such importance in those societies.

Under capitalism, the economic base has control. Economics dominates. Structures and superstructures establish relations of production (which in no way eliminates delays, discrepancies, or disparities). Conflicts themselves are the result of relations of production. To the extent that this society possesses any coherence at all (without which it would break apart into pieces or, rather, without which it could not have been formed), to the extent that internal cohesion, although it cannot eliminate contradictions, manages to attenuate or postpone their effects, there is a "mode of production" and even a "system." The wealth of societies "in which the capitalist mode of production prevails" appears as an immense accumulation of commodities. Thus, *Capital* begins with a reference to an earlier "critique of political economy." With the rise of the bourgeoisie, exchange value conquered use and use value; it treated them as servants, as slaves. The origin of the need the object satisfied mattered little, whether it arose from the stomach or the imagination, as long as the object could be bought and sold. The bourgeoisie invented political economy; it is its condition, its means of action, its ideological and scientific milieu. Consequently, it is on this terrain, its own, that it must be attacked. This demands courage and entails risks, like any combat on enemy territory; in combating these postulates, we risk allowing ourselves to be influenced by them. Nevertheless, *historical categories* are subordinate to *economic categories*. The gravity of this situation and any theoretical decisions it required explain Marx's hesitation; he had to take into account the failure of the revolution of 1848 and the rapid rise of capitalism in Europe, signaling a victory of the economic over the historical. The critique of political economy is carried out neither by history nor in the name of history (as becoming or as science). It must occur within political economy; the revolutionary act must explode the *system* from within (which implies contradictions within the relations of production, first of all, and then between relations of production and the *mode of production*).

From this perspective, in this light, the city provides the background; against this background occur many events and notable facts, which analysis detaches from a relatively uniform background. The city is there all the time, a scene in which economic categories, wages and capital, surplus product and surplus value, play out their storylines and their dramas. Against this background, thought takes up relatively little space. From time to time, as void or emergence, the historical background suddenly moves to the foreground. It presents certain problems.

Isn't this the intent of the well-known methodological fragment with which the *Grundrisse* opens? "When we consider a given country politico-economically, we begin with its population, its distribution among classes, town, country, the coast, the different branches of production, export and import, annual production and consumption, commodity prices etc." (100). Not without intentional disorder, however, because, ironically, Marx enumerates what the common economist counts, for the economist is content to describe and, consequently, justify what exists, assuming it to be a "fait accompli." We cannot, however, overlook the facts, even though our findings may appear to be insufficiently thought through. "It seems to be correct to begin with the real and the concrete." But we soon discover the error. For, if we accept this, we confuse the concrete and the immediate, knowledge and description, the real and the given. "The population is an abstraction if I leave out, for example, the classes of which it is composed. These classes in turn are an empty phrase if I am not familiar with the elements on which they rest. E.g. wage labor, capital, etc. These latter in turn presuppose exchange, division of labor, prices, etc." (ibid.). Therefore, the concrete method will begin with abstractions, but scientific abstractions: *abstract general relations,* such as the division of labor, value, money. Based on these concepts, whose content consists of relations, thinking will attempt to *generate the concrete* (and which will achieve this concrete, a product of thought, by defining it, rather than presenting it as a given).

The method *generates* the linking of concepts at the same time as the concepts themselves. By examining their differences, it rediscovers the content initially overlooked by the reduction that eliminates chaotic vision, replacing description with analysis. Thus, based on the general concept of *labor,* we discover the role and even the representation of productive labor in different societies (including the United States and Russia, cf. 105). We generate the concept of the city, of its relation to the countryside, of their conflicts and the modalities of those conflicts (107).

In this way is the critique of political economy—immanent to political economy as reality, inherent in political economy as science—developed. The method is not restricted to a critique of *bourgeois* political economy; it shows how all political economy is fundamentally bourgeois. It provides a critique of all political economy, just as the Marxist critique of the state is valid for any state, not just the bourgeois state. For every state is a class state, that of the dominant class; this apparatus enables it to *mask* its contradictions through ideology, to *suppress* the consequences through force.

This approach has various implications: the end of political economy, inseparable from the end of exchange (and the use that stands in opposition to exchange)—the end of work (and leisure)—the end of the town (and the countryside). But it does entail certain complications.

4

Engels and Utopia

I want now to examine the role, albeit a small one, played by Engels's *The Housing Question*. This slender volume comprises three articles Engels wrote in 1872 "when the blessing of the French milliards was pouring over Germany: ... when Germany was entering the world arena not only a 'united empire,' but also as a great industrial country."[1]

It has become customary to present this collection as the last word on Marxist thought concerning urban questions. Apparently, merely citing *The Housing Question* frees us from the need to read it or understand its theoretical structure. But these texts have a very clear circumstantial character; and although Engels's preface from 1887 corrects this and gives greater scope to the book, it also adds to the confusion. On several occasions, Engels uses the term "industrial revolution" without any further explanation when discussing events that transpired in Germany during these years (which also saw Marx's death).

Engels and his companion in struggle found themselves facing a twofold problem: the duration of capitalism and the rise of the workers' movement. They had announced the coming end of the capitalist mode of production; and, as late as 1887, Engels was imprudent enough to repeat the prophecy. As for the workers' movement, it took on a political form, which surprised Engels, as it had Marx on more than one occasion. They realized, and were alone in this realization, that the state and its most skillful rulers (Bismarck) would attempt to co-opt the workers' movement and integrate the working class into bourgeois society. From that moment on, theoretical thought and political action split. There were "right-wingers" and "left-wingers"; on the one hand, Proudhon and Lassalle and their followers, the Proudhonians and Lassalleans, and, on the other, Bakuninists and anarchists. Marx and Engels were forced to fight on two fronts, especially after the failure of the Commune, a failure that fully revealed the revolutionary scope of the events in Paris. Although occupying a "central" position, Engels and Marx refused to define a type of "centrism," refused to indicate a middle way, to accept compromise. It is remarkable that they lashed out primarily against the right, directing their strongest blows at the "opportunists," Lassalle and Proudhon, and against the brilliant—and seemingly "left-wing"— formulas they employed to mask their concessions to society as it existed.

Given the conditions in Germany in 1872, it is ridiculous to present as revolutionary the project to abolish rent or construct working-class housing with the help of the state. Such projects, for Engels as well as for Marx, directly served Bismarck's state and the perpetuation of capitalist social relations. "The housing shortage from which the workers and part of the petty bourgeoisie suffer in our modern big cities is one of the numerous *smaller,* secondary evils which result from the present-day capitalist mode of production. It is not at all a direct result of the exploitation of the worker as a worker by the capitalists. This exploitation is the basic evil which the social revolution strives to abolish by abolishing the capitalist mode of production" (22). Engels shows that there is always a "housing shortage" for the oppressed and the exploited and that the housing question cannot be resolved by the bourgeoisie; it would nonetheless be a serious error to consider it essential.

For Engels, the housing question is merely a subordinate aspect of a central problem, that of the relations between town and country or, rather, that of overcoming their opposition. Those who suggest building housing for the workers and transferring the housing to the workers are not satisfied with fictively resolving the "social question" by transforming workers into capitalists; they want to introduce the "cottage system" and worker dormitories, organizing them so as to do as little harm as possible. This reformism contains an avowal. "On its own admission, therefore, the bourgeois solution of the housing question has come to grief—it has come to grief owing to the *antithesis of town and country*. And with this we have arrived at the kernel of the problem. The housing question can only be solved when society has been sufficiently transformed for a start to be made towards abolishing the antithesis between town and country, which has been brought to an extreme point by present-day capitalist society. Far from being able to abolish this antithesis, capitalist society on the contrary is compelled to intensify it day by day" (54). So, for Engels, in 1872, neither the cottage (today we might call it a suburban house) nor the dormitory (we would say "subsidized housing") can make headway against the fundamental problem, which is not that of housing. And this holds true even if we were to multiply the available housing until such "needs" are met. This objective itself is of a reformist nature for it eludes and obscures the problem of revolutionary transformation. "On the other hand the first modern utopian socialists, Owen and Fourier, already correctly recognized this. In their model plans the antithesis between town and country no longer exists" (ibid.).

Engels refers here to utopian, or revolutionary, socialism as opposed to a reformist and reactionary utopia, which, although more "utopian," dissimulates the problem rather than bringing it to light. "[The housing shortage] cannot fail to be present in a society in which the great masses of the workers are exclusively dependent upon wages, that is to say, on the sum of foodstuffs necessary for their existence and for the propagation of their kind; in which improvements of the existing machinery continually throw masses of workers out of employment; in which violent and regularly recurring industrial vacillations determine on the one hand the existence of a large reserve army of unemployed workers, and on the other hand drive large masses of the workers temporarily unemployed onto the streets; in which the workers are crowded together in masses in the big towns, at a quicker rate than dwellings come into existence for them under existing conditions; in which, therefore, there must always be tenants even for the most infamous pigsties; and in which finally the house owner in his capacity as capitalist has not only the right, but, in view of the competition, to a certain extent also the duty of ruthlessly making as much out of his property in house rent as he possibly can. In such a society the housing shortage is no accident; it is a necessary institution" (46–47).

After having evoked (or invoked) Fourier and while continuing his polemic against Proudhon, Engels reminds us that actual conditions *prevent* (rather than simply hinder) overcoming the opposition. But reactionary utopianism provides an image of the future that preserves these conditions while portraying life and society as something different. Thus, Proudhon claims "to transform present-day bourgeois society while maintaining the peasant as such" (96). As for revolutionary utopianism, it possesses a "wonderful practical foundation" when we observe that, every day, London discards, at great expense, more natural fertilizer than Saxony produces, so that an illustrious savant by the name of Liebig asks that man shall give back to the earth what he takes from it, "in which he proves that only the existence of the towns, and in particular the big towns, prevents this" (95). The suppression of the opposition between town and country is no more a utopia (abstract) than the suppression of the antagonism between capital and wages. In fact, it becomes an increasingly "practical necessity."

It is even more interesting to listen to Engels when he defends *urbanity* together with the cultural heritage that is transmitted historically and worth preserving. "There never were greater boors than our modern bourgeois" (30). Engels himself appears satisfied that he has been able to show that "[he] can prove that the production of our modern society is sufficient to provide all its members with enough to eat, and that there are houses enough in existence to provide the working masses for the time being with roomy and healthy living accommodation" (101).

Let us now turn to the *Anti-Dühring* (1878), a magisterial work par excellence, a compendium and encyclopedia, a perpetual reference, Holy Book and Vulgate, and an abundant source of citations.[2] In others words, the most controversial, most severely criticized, as well as the most read and discussed work of Marxist literature, along with Lenin's *Materialism and Empirio-Criticism*.

Marxist unitarians and dogmatists stubbornly insist on the coherence of the system. They transform Marxist theory into a doctrine or "system" in the traditional (philosophical) sense of the term. This harmonizes well with its political transformation into a state ideology, cultural pedagogy, and institutional practice. But here and elsewhere, the accent has been on Engels's originality, on the specificity of his contribution, his particular approach to revolutionary thought. We could just as easily speak of "Engelsism" as we could of "Lassalleism" or "Leninism" as different and, often, divergent currents of contemporary thought within the revolutionary movement. This does not, of course, exclude other differences.

In *Anti-Dühring,* Engels is clear about orienting revolutionary thought, Marx's as well as his own, toward philosophy and nature. He gives it a *cosmological* content and is clear about systematizing it in that direction. But why? Well, but why not? Some have argued that he did so to be fully in agreement with Marx. This is possible, but it would seem that Marx's objectives did not exactly coincide with those of Engels. When he examined the "naturalist" thinkers and scientific works (especially those on electricity and its applications), he did so to understand the energy and information exchange between society and nature rather than to derive a *philosophia naturalis,* a "conception of the world." There is nothing analogous in Marx to the "dialectical materialism" developed by Engels and later Lenin.

Anti-Dühring compares one system with another. Polemics of this nature are often risky—the more forceful the attack, the more they venture forth onto the enemy's terrain. So how does Dühring come off in the dispute? Who was he? A robust intellect, a man who constructed a nonnegligible system notwithstanding the contempt showered upon him by Engels (which recalls Marx's contempt for Stirner and Proudhon). Dühring didn't lack for rigor or range. The unfairness of the majority of Marxist exegetes and epigones in this regard lapses into derision. Would Engels have wasted his time and effort in attacking an unimportant adversary? In deprecating Dühring, like Stirner or Proudhon, by considering them to be ideological corpses, we belittle Marx and Engels; we present them as the executioners of great works of history, the hangmen of thought. A strange philosophy hides behind this vulgar authoritarianism. In truth, Eugen Dühring was a kind of *structuralist avant la lettre,* a methodical and rigorous thinker who classified and identified and separated instead of connecting and highlighting (dialectical) transitions. For our purposes, and with more general implications, Dühring represented *the separation of town and country as a permanent structure of societies.* This position had serious consequences and explains Engels's opprobrium without in any way justifying the posthumous contempt. Engels clearly perceived the inherent dogmatism in Dühring's thinking when he cites, in his preliminary notes, a significant passage and accompanies it with a highly expressive gloss. "A 'new mode of thought' and its results are 'from the foundation upwards original conclusions and views . . . system-creating ideas . . . established truths.' In it we have before us 'a work which must find its strength in concentrated initiative'—whatever that may mean; an 'investigation going to the roots . . . a deep-rooted science . . . ; a strictly scientific conception of things and of men . . . an all-round penetrating work of thought . . . a creative scheme of hypotheses and deductions controllable by thought . . . the absolute fundamental basis'" (45), Dühring wrote in his preface to a course of political economy (1876). Engels, who copied this text, added "And the future has to follow this direction" (46). The remainder of Engels's notes illustrate how and why he wants to crush this abstract, systematic antidialectical scientificity, which separates thought from the culture of nature and cancels history by hypothesis and decree. This dogmatic attitude attempts to hide behind an apology for violence. Only pure and unfettered violence can modify "structures" that are inherently fixed, even necessary, and possibly eternal, because, according to Dühring, his thought exchanges "the confusion of generally nebulous ideas with the meaning of the appropriate disjunction and the strict discrimination of actual elements of processes."

For Engels, the first great division of labor was that between town and country; for Dühring, this antagonism was inevitable—"in the nature of things" (398)—especially because he discerned "a constancy of interconnection" between them (ibid.) and because of trade and industry (especially alcohol, Engels sarcastically notes).

Against the separation achieved by Dühring in the name of scientific rigor between town and country, Engels remarks that the elimination of this state "is not a utopia," although civilization, in our large cities, has left us with a heritage that will require a great deal of time and effort to eliminate. The childish idea, an abstract and vain utopia, is one that sees society as capable of taking possession of all the means of production "without abolishing the former division of labor." This assumption Engels attributes to Dühring and his Prussian socialism, notwithstanding his apology for revolutionary violence. Dühring sees nothing better in the future than the redistribution of urban populations, based on technologies for the best use of raw materials, that is, according to "social needs" (399). But for what society? Why, the one that exists, of course: one based on the capitalist mode of production.

Engels, reacting to this disturbing reformism with its "audacious" phraseology, once more reaches out to his inspiration and secret weapon—Fourier. To that end, we again note the extent to which dogmatism falsified Engels's thought as well as that of Marx by relegating the French utopian socialists to the shadows, especially Fourier. For Engels, Owen and Fourier complement each other. The English take into account large-scale industry and the French the multitude of acts associated with life, work, and enjoyment. "The utopians were already perfectly clear in their minds as to the effects of the division of labor" (402). Concerning this important point, Engels and Marx are in complete agreement. The revolution is not defined by the elimination of the bourgeoisie as a political class but by overturning the socioeconomic relations that constitute the armature of bourgeois society. The separation of town and country is part of it. The revolutionary project, that of general overcoming, pushes this partial overcoming to the foreground; it therefore ceases to be a historical category, which is itself surpassed. To escape this capitalist impasse, to do away with the priority of the economic, there is one, and only one, possibility: eliminating the division of labor. "The abolition of the antithesis between town and country was demanded by Fourier, as by Owen, as the first prerequisite for the abolition of the old division of labor altogether" (ibid.). Although the great utopians were utopians, this does not imply that their arguments were ineffectual, far from it. It simply meant that the realization of the revolutionary project was not yet possible. But large-scale industry supplied the conditions, together with "the contradictions lying dormant in the capitalist mode of production into such crying antagonisms that the approaching collapse of this mode of production is, so to speak, palpable; that the new productive forces themselves can only be maintained and further developed by the introduction of a new mode of production corresponding to their present stage of development" (363). This Dühring ignores just as he misinterprets Owen and Fourier, whose romantic fantasies alone he is familiar with, whereas on each page of Fourier "the sparks of reason burst forth."

Engels wasn't satisfied with comparing socialist utopianism to bourgeois utopianism; he contrasted *revolutionary and concrete utopia* with reactionary and abstract utopia. Concrete utopia is based on the movement of a reality whose possibilities it discovers. Dialectically, the possible is a category of reality once we consider its *tendencies* in the real rather than assigning it a fixed place.

However, the modern reader, who no longer follows the structures of dogmatism, wonders if Engels has fully described his concept and his project. Sometimes, he appears to come out against any utopia whatsoever. "It is not utopian to declare that the emancipation of humanity from the chains which its historic past has forged will only be complete when the antithesis between town and country has been abolished; the utopia begins when one undertakes 'from existing conditions' to prescribe the form in which this or any other of the antitheses of present-day society is to be solved."[3] For which he reproaches the Proudhonians! This text, among others, serves as a reference for those who oppose any utopia and any form of utopianism. If that is the case, we can accuse Engels of inconsistency when he makes use of the "utopian" propositions of Fourier and Owen. "Both of them thought that the population should be scattered through the country in groups of sixteen hundred to three thousand persons; each group was to occupy a gigantic palace, run on communal lines, in the center of their area of land. It is true that Fourier occasionally refers to towns, but these were only to consist in turn of four or five such palaces situated near each other."[4] Unquestionably, Engels anticipates the form of supersession based on existing conditions. The city will disappear. It must disappear. Engels had formed this idea in his youth and never abandoned it. In *The Housing Question,* he already predicted the "abolition of the capitalist mode of production" and assumed an equitable distribution of the population throughout the country.[5] The solution to urban problems excludes keeping the large modern cities. Engels doesn't appear to ask himself if this dispersion of the city into the countryside, in the form of small communities, doesn't risk dissolving "urbanity," of ruralizing urban reality. Nor does he ask whether this "equal distribution" corresponds to the requirements of large-scale industry. In this sense, the multiplicity of possible communications provides a sufficient response. It is quite clear that Engels's attachment to Fourierist thought, an impassioned and perfectly understandable attachment as such and so well expressed a half-century earlier (see *The German Ideology*), prevents him from asking certain questions. Fifty years later, his attitude will have consequences of extreme gravity in the USSR.[6]

Anti-Dühring has its good points and its bad, and the dialectical thought displayed sometimes defies logic (social and political). It opens with a view to the future and the possible, while at the same time systematizing and closing off the system. It attempts to establish an ontology, an answer to such questions as "What is being? What is the human being? Where does he come from? Where is he going?" But the answers oscillate between a science that is confident of its success and an uncertain exploration of the future. The concept of nature dominates it all. To restore society and, therefore, the "urban," as we would call it, in nature, seen as a context and, better yet, as source and original depth, wouldn't this be the sense of Engels's project and its Fourierist inspiration? Here too, the controversy has drawn Engels onto enemy territory. He fought Schelling, the romantic philosopher of nature, the thinker par excellence of an ontological foundation sought within the original: the grandmother, the womb. Engels doesn't want to cut the umbilical cord; nor does he want it to dry out. For him, the exchange must continue, it must remain or become organic once more. Doesn't he find both Marx and Fourier to be in fundamental agreement?

This immediately leads to several other questions. Are these implicit or explicit affinities essential to Marxist thought? Should we, today, focus on them or on the revolutionary nature of large-scale industry? Although the thesis of a perpetual living relation between the social and the natural may harbor an essential truth, isn't it already too late? From where does the failure (at least, apparent) of this truth arise? Doesn't modernism consist of the transgression, possibly even the destruction, of this truth? Should we conceptualize urban society using the arguments of Marx and

Engels or transgress those arguments, or update them, or find something else?

Attentive rereading of Engels's great work in a way confirms these perplexities. His systematization, guided by the concept of nature (perhaps the only one able to explicitly or implicitly determine a philosophical system), erases certain distinctions noted by Marx, certain differences indicated by him. Political economy, "the science of the laws governing the production and exchange of the material means of subsistence in human society," no longer implies its opposite: the critique of political economy.[7] All ages, all societies, all modes of production have an economic "basis," which, for Engels, appears to explain them. Unlike Marx, he does not distinguish historical categories (concepts) from economic categories (concepts). Political economy and history are mixed to the point of confusion, for political economy "deals with material which is historical, that is, constantly changing; it must first investigate the special laws of each individual stage in the evolution of production and exchange, and only when it has completed this investigation will it be able to establish the few quite general laws which hold good for production and exchange in general" (204). In contrast to philosophy, the history of philosophy, and history in general, for Engels everything is economic. History is absorbed into political economy; the revolutionary project, viewed as a release from the economic, loses its meaning and scope, even though it preserves them in terms of the division of labor.

The first consequence is that the history of the city, as viewed by Engels, does not receive the same treatment as it does in the *Grundrisse*. With his emphasis on urban concentrations, Engels associates the history of the city with that of technology, arms, and armed struggle: "From the outset, therefore, firearms were the weapons of the towns, and of the rising town-supported monarchy against the feudal nobility" (231). Because of this, and simultaneously, infantry replaced cavalry as the principal armed force: during the Middle Ages, in the towns and among the free peasants, the basic conditions for a seasoned infantry were created.[8] It was through the towns, therefore, that "the silent labor of the oppressed masses" destroyed, then swept away, the feudal order. In the fifteenth century, the bourgeoisie of the towns had become more essential to society than the feudal nobility. The needs of the nobility itself had grown and been transformed to the point that, even for the nobility, the towns had become indispensable.

The transition from the original community (of blood, family, or custom) to the urban commune, its rise and transition from dominated reality to dominant reality, the lengthy conflict between town and country, are only touched upon by Engels. Marx, however, in the *Grundrisse,* analyzed them in detail, taking into account the variety of differences and situations in this (general) historical process. Engels did enrich and enlarge his economic analysis with his views on armed struggle. He fought the unconditional apology for violence found in Dühring by situating it historically as the midwife to society. The great medieval revolution, that of the serfs and communes, with which European history begins, is found in Engels in all its magnitude, as a struggle that is variously seen as extensive, silent, or bloody. Engels's emphasis on the economic does not lead to economism. It is paradoxical that it may have been Marx who, in pursuing the dialectical critique of political economy, did not sufficiently insist on actual struggles and represented them, rather, as part of a process of nearly spontaneous organic growth. Engels outlined the process and showed, dialectically, the conflicts that ultimately lead to the paroxysm of war.

But there was a second, more surprising consequence. When Marx pushed his theoretical reasoning as far as it could go, where did he go and what did he find? The reign of ends. Among those ends and surrounding them, or assuming them, beyond any partial ends, if we can call them that (the end of state capitalism, of scarcity, of philosophy, of history, of the family, and so on), we previously noted that of *labor*. The end of labor was a paradox for the man who had discovered the importance of labor and was assumed, above all else, to be the theoretician of the working class. And yet, we already know that the automation of production helps us to foresee the end of productive labor. Is this a theoretical and practical possibility? Absolutely. The subsequent linking of technical discoveries has fully confirmed Marx's views. Is it an impossibility? Certainly, among the proponents of capitalism and even during the well-known "transition" to a socialist or communist society. It is, therefore, a utopia, but a *concrete utopia,* a possibility that illuminates the actual and which the actual isolates in impossibility. In our sense, one of the greatest strengths of Marxist thought—impossible to reduce, difficult to "co-opt"—resides in this act of looking forward carried out by Marx in the mid-nineteenth century. *The only meaning, the only goal that can be given to work is nonwork.* Alongside this proposition, established on a solid foundation, we find that the critique of political economy and the failures of a socialism that claims to be Marxist are not very significant. Can it cast a new light on the future, on urban reality, on the transcendence of town and country? Possibly, as a point of departure for a new search. But what I want to emphasize here is that Engels overlooked the paradox of the future. What is it that limits and imprisons his thought? His tendency to systematization? Ontology? Naturalism? The seductions of Fourierism? These are not mutually exclusive. It is the case, however, that Engels does not foresee overcoming the division of labor by nonlabor (the end of labor) but of making work free and appealing. "The old mode of production must therefore be revolutionized from top to bottom, and in particular the former division of labor must disappear. Its place must be taken by an organization of production . . . in which, therefore, productive labor will become a pleasure instead of a burden" (403–4). The socialization of productive forces, the elimination of restrictions, disturbances, and waste enables us to reduce labor time and metamorphize labor. "This is no longer a fantasy, no longer a pious wish." Civilization, inevitably distinct from society for centuries, will rejoin it once more. A society that humanely organizes its productive forces "on the basis of one single vast plan," can undertake this transformation and "allow industry to be distributed over the whole country in the way best adapted to its own development and to the maintenance and development, of the other elements of production" (407). And it is with this that Engels's thought rediscovers its disavowed utopianism and cohesion. And here too that he differs, for better or for worse, from his audacious companion, from the Marxist "finality" of long-term utopianism.

5

Capital and Land Ownership

From the *Grundrisse* to *Capital,* the picture changes, but not in any simple way. The methodological and theoretical insights found in the *Grundrisse* confirm this, although in a somewhat disorderly fashion. Critical knowledge, which for Marx constitutes true science (free of ideology), has found its beginning; it knows where and how to proceed, what to criticize. Yet, there is a definite loss: differences are not as forcefully highlighted, they are less strongly emphasized and elaborated. On the other hand, there is greater rigor in the chain of reasoning, and this is already present at the start of the book: *pure form.*

Capital begins with generalities, following the methodological process of the *Grundrisse,* but they are not quite the same. The generalities found in the *Grundrisse* are *contents,* treated as generalities in thought: production, the level of production, the way in which members of a society adapt (fashion) natural objects based on their needs, and so on. These generalities borrowed from content are not false; they are, however, trivial. Such banalities fail to escape the seesawing between *subject* (mankind, the individual, society) and *system* (the connection between production and consumption, between needs and satisfactions, between objects and subjects, between structures and functions).

Capital—I repeat—starts explicitly from a *form,* completely purified (through reduction) of all content. A subtle abstraction of nearly theological difficulty, although highly scientific in nature, doesn't it define the very essence of scientific thought itself for Marx? "Beginnings are always difficult in all sciences. The understanding of the first chapter, especially the section that contains the analysis of commodities, will therefore present the greatest difficulty. I have popularized the passages concerning the substance of value and the magnitude of value as much as possible. *The value-form, whose fully developed shape is the money-form,* is very simple and slight in content. Nevertheless, the human mind has sought in vain for more than two thousand years to get to the bottom of it, . . . With the exception of the section on the *form of value,* therefore, this volume cannot stand accused on the score of difficulty. I assume, of course, a reader who is willing to learn something new and therefore to think for himself. . . . What I have to examine in this work is the *capitalist mode of production,* and *the relations of production and forms of intercourse [Verkehrsverhältnisse]* that correspond to it."[1]

We have apparently lost the town–country theme, their social relation, and the problems this presents. But the separation is more apparent than real. This relation is part of the content the initial reduction sets aside, a reduction that isolates the pure form of social relations: the form of exchange. Yet, if the author of *Capital* lives up to his commitment, he must, at the conclusion of a certain theoretical trajectory, rediscover the considered relation, while *generating* it, while *situating* it, as social relation, in the *mode of production,* itself considered as a whole; a cohesiveness that is nonetheless subject to the forces of separation, anticohesion, and *supersession.* Starting from the "purest," the simplest beginning, *subjects* (to the extent that they exist) and *systems* (to the extent that they too exist), *functions* and *structures* must be found, and clarified over the course of their genesis.

More than half a century ago, Lenin claimed that no one had really read and understood *Capital,* having failed to assimilate Hegelian dialectics. According to Lenin, the necessary conceptual equipment was lacking in readers of Marx's great work. Fifty years later, one might wonder whether the conceptual equipment doesn't sin from excess. We arrive at Marx, our mind stuffed with interpretations; we question him, and immediately substitute whatever comes into our heads rather than what he says. This results in a so-called symptomatic reading. A literal reading would unquestionably be better, providing it avoids the methods of those superannuated orthodox commentators who dig up the Marxist landscape hoping to extract quotations, invariably the same.

This is not the place to again discuss the method used in *Capital* or how it should be read. It is more important to trace its movement, to follow its development through to the end. Marx thought it worthwhile, not without reason, to begin with the more rarefied form, to the extent that it comes very close to a completely "pure" form, a logical form, the form studied by formal logic.[2] This form of the exchange of material objects is also similar to verbal exchange and communication, language. It enables Marx to illustrate the connections it implies in an (almost) purely logical manner. It also enables him to develop, from this beginning, a theoretical discourse, an interlinking of concepts intended to account for all of capitalist society, down to the smallest detail, while also taking into account—and appropriately positioning—various aspects of content: from social labor to the family, from the enterprise to the nation, from surplus value to the town–country relationship, and so on.

In Marx's approach, this theoretical discourse combines knowledge and revolution. It supplies the theoretical knowledge of bourgeois society and political economy (capitalist by definition), a knowledge that is both critical and concrete. It *is* the theoretical revolution. In doing so, it encounters the trivial discourse of daily life and the world of commodities, that of the capitalist individual, along with the corresponding modalities of consciousness, theoretical knowledge, and ideology. In the process, it dissipates those signifieds to establish a rational sequence of signifiers that does not coincide with the "real" as it appears to those who are immersed in this real, but which clarifies it by transforming it from an opaque reality to a transparent reality, exposed to the action that will destroy it.

This theoretical discourse against ideology assumes (according to Marx, apparently) no special competence. To follow it, one need only know how to interlink its concepts and abstract from them. Although Lenin overestimates this know-how by claiming that Marx was accessible only to serious dialecticians, we can also assume, conversely, that the hypothesis by which conceptual interlinking and the interlinking of words in spoken language are close to one another, is a bit too optimistic.

Let's approach this somewhat differently to illustrate its orientation. Let us assume that there is someone with common sense and, therefore, an "empiricist," who attempts to comprehend what's going on around him. He'll count objects, things: this table, this bed, this butter, this sugar, and so on, or these houses, these streets, these buildings. He'll draw up a list of objects. Continuing his research, he will ask the price of those objects; in stores he could read the labels on the things he finds useful in his life; and he will keep his list of objects and prices up to date. Next, he will determine the needs that the properties of those things satisfy. After doing so, according to Marx, he will be able to write a treaty on political economy (in the common rather than the critical meaning of the term); this will be an apology of the society as it exists. But nowhere, at no time, will this "scholar" (who may, in actuality, know a great many things!) have grasped any *relation* among *objects,* among monetary units. He will have counted and grouped them, considering them one by one. He will not know why or how an object might "be worth" a certain amount of money and he will never learn that he doesn't know. Even less will he learn how and why *two objects* (or several) can be worth *the same amount of money* and, conversely, how and why an *object* can be worth several different amounts of money whenever its price changes. He will have seen no more than *economic facts,* nowhere a *social relation.*

Marx, however, describes social relations. First of all, the "thing," the object, contains an initial relation. It is doubled, there, before our eyes, even though the "form of exchange" does not initially indicate that it is a "polarized form," containing oppositions within itself. Only analysis can bring to light what is before our eyes; only knowledge can *reveal* this thing. It implies *use value* and *exchange value*. Use value corresponds to need, to expectation, to desirability. Exchange value corresponds to the relation of that thing to other things, to all objects and all things in the "world of commodities."

This world of commodities has its own logic, its own language, which theoretical discourse encounters and "understands" (consequently dissipating its illusions). Because it has internal consistency, this world wants to spontaneously (automatically) expand without limits; and it can. It covers the entire world; it's the global market. Everything can be bought and sold, evaluated in monetary terms. Every function and structure created by it becomes part of this world and supports it. Yet, that world never manages to achieve closure. Its consistency has limits; its pretentions will disappoint those who gamble on exchange and the value of exchange as an absolute. For a commodity escapes the world of commodities: labor or, rather, the laborer's (proletarian's) labor time. He sells his *labor time* and remains—in principle—free; even if he believes he has sold his labor and himself, he has rights, capabilities, powers that weaken the absolute domination of the world of commodities over the entire world. Through this breach other "values" can enter: use value, relations of free association, and so on. This is not a temporary breach, however, for the contradiction establishes itself in the heart of capitalism's cohesion.

Surplus value appears on several levels. First, at the level of the individual worker: during the labor time he provides the capitalist, he produces more than he receives in the form of money in his salary; this difference constitutes the social *productivity* of labor. Such is the structure of capitalism. Second, at the enterprise or branch level of industry, capitalists receive their share of overall surplus value based on the amount of capital invested, to the extent that the tendency to form an average rate of profit functions. Third, with respect to society as a whole, that is, the state, it absorbs a significant share of overall surplus value (using different methods:

taxes, state-run enterprises) and acts powerfully on its distribution among the various class layers and fractions of bourgeois society. In particular, it manages the large-scale public services that are essential to a society and make up that society, although they do not coincide with the economic production–consumption relation, which is the basis of bourgeois society. These include such things as schools and universities, transportation, health care and hospitals, "culture," and, *consequently, the city.*

Capital examines, in succession:

(a) *The formation of surplus value* by labor and surplus labor (which enables capital to be accumulated). Capitalists in general and each capitalist in particular struggle to increase their profits, that is, their share of surplus value, by various means: extension of the workday, increased productivity, technical or organizational improvements, acceleration of the flow of capital. This presents them with difficult problems, especially those involving overproduction.

(b) *The realization of surplus value.* It is essential that the M-C-M (money, commodities, money) circuit be completed and secured as quickly as possible. Money, which has acquired the status of capital, is invested. Labor, thus engaged, produces commodities; those commodities must be reconverted into money, that is, they must be sold for there to be a profit. To sell and to sell for a profit (surplus value), this concern hounds the individual capitalist, spurs on capitalists and their managers, and as a class endows them with a kind of genius. Every capitalist would like to free himself of this implacable necessity, wishing only that his money should produce money directly. This can occur through speculation (real estate, stock trading, and so on). But only some capital experiences this welcome fate; a sufficient excess in this direction and the system goes off the rails. Overall, capitalism and capitalists must continue the process without end, the marvelous *circulus vitiosus* (M-C-M-C-M, and so on). It's their Sisyphean rock.

(c) *The distribution of surplus value.* Every capitalist makes use of his invested capital like a pump that sucks up surplus value in bulk. Only in appearance does the capitalist exploit "his" workers and employees. In truth, the class of capitalists, that is, the bourgeoisie, exploits *society as a whole,* including non-proletarians, peasants, employees, and so on; but primarily and directly, the proletariat. The mass of surplus value is distributed among *these various sectors,* including landowners, merchants, the so-called liberal professions, and so on. This distribution occurs on a general level. The state monitors its progress in order to prevent sudden shocks to the system. On the other hand, it removes a considerable share of surplus value, through taxes primarily, to keep society going, to support the development of skills and education, the army and police, the bureaucracy and culture. We know that the capitalist state invests very little money in culture, for the bourgeoisie believes only in its economic foundations; moreover, it supports only those aspects of culture that can be used and integrated into bourgeois society. *Social needs* are met by the capitalist state solely on the basis of the needs of the bourgeoisie. The contractual (legal) system that the state maintains and perfects in the form of (political) power relies on *private property,* that of land (fixed assets) and money (personal assets).

These interlinked analyses compose a complete (critical) exposé of bourgeois society and capitalism. The rational and, consequently, revolutionary (according to Marx) discourse extends from its logical beginnings to its opposite pole: the operation of bourgeois society. The concrete—social practice—is discovered at the conclusion of the process; it is present at the start as a text to be deciphered and at the end as a known totality (decoded, as some modern thinkers might say). But most readers, especially "scholarly" readers, only look for what they are comfortable with—and find it, sometimes at the beginning of the work (the theory of commodities and commodity fetishism), sometimes further on (the theory of classes), but rarely at the end, in the theory of social totality and its inherent tendencies (toward monopolistic concentration of capital or toward the predominance of a rationality of planning that rests on the action of the working class).

Here, I want to point out another aspect of *Capital* that presents a certain difficulty—in spite of its scope, the work remains incomplete. The theory with which the work was supposed to culminate, the *distribution of surplus value,* leaves the reader hungry for more, as they say. The book fails to clearly present either the "subjects" (classes and class fractions) or the existing mode of production in place (clearly defined as such), or the systems and subsystems it comprises (legal, fiscal, contractual, and so on). Why should this incompleteness concern us? Because, and most importantly, the Marxist theory of land ownership under capitalism is incomplete. How and why does a class of landowners perpetuate itself under capitalism, where movable (personal) property strongly predominates? How does land rent originate? What does it imply? The question comprises agriculture, grazing, mining, water, and, of course, the *built domain* of cities. Concerning this point, whose importance we cannot overstate, we need to identify Marx's insights and interpret them as a whole.

But now, let us return to the city. The concept of the city, as such, belongs to history; it is a *historical category.* However, as we already know, the analysis and exposé of capitalism include history and historical categories but subordinate them to economic and economic categories (concepts). Such an approach is based on the internal structure of capitalism itself. Economic categories, therefore, "bear a historical stamp," because "definite historical conditions are involved in the existence of the product as a commodity."[3] There is nothing natural about the relation between those who possess money or commodities and those who possess their labor power alone, nor is it a relation that is shared throughout all periods of history. It is obviously the result of a historical development and even of a number of revolutions that destroyed earlier forms. "Although we come across the first sporadic traces of capitalist production as early as the fourteenth or fifteenth centuries in certain towns of the Mediterranean, the capitalist era dates from the sixteenth century. Wherever it appears, the abolition of serfdom has long since been completed, and the most brilliant achievement of the Middle Ages, the existence of independent city-states, has already been on the wane for a considerable length of time."[4] But history alone does not explain these relations, their forms or formation.

The city, as such, is part of those historical conditions, which are involved in the growth of capitalism. It results from the destruction of earlier social formations and the primitive accumulation of capital (which is accomplished in it and by it). It is a *social thing*, in which are noticeable to the senses (become perceptible) social relations that, in and of themselves, are not noticeable to the senses, so that they must be conceptualized by thought based on their concrete (practical) realization. In this context, that of social relations, the circulation of commodities and the creation of trade and the market, the starting point for capital in the sixteenth century, take place. Here, the "magic of money" is at work, the marvelous and stupidly brutal power of things—gold and silver—taken from the belly of the earth, which become the embodiment of human labor (128). In the city, the world of commodities, abstract in itself (because consisting of relations detached from use), encounters nature, simulates it, can appear natural, passes off its material embodiment as natural. The requirements of capital and the needs of the bourgeoisie are assumed to be both natural and social ("cultural" we would say today). Shaped by history in the urban context, such needs become essential. Thus, "In contrast, therefore, with the case of other commodities, the determination of the value of labor-power contains a historical and moral element" (275). The so-called natural needs, their number and manner of satisfaction, depend "to a great extent on the level of civilization attained by a country" (ibid.). Under capitalism, in spite of the outsized hopes of individual capitalists, this limits the exploitation of labor power: "the extension of the working day encounters moral obstacles. The worker needs time in which to satisfy his intellectual and social requirements, and the extent and the number of these requirements is conditioned by the general level of civilization" (341). We should take note, for we will encounter it later on, of this concept of *civilization,* which Marx distinguishes from *society* (which achieves a more or less elevated degree of civilization), as well as the constituent social-economic relations. Civilization is not separated from society, which simultaneously determines and limits civilization. The predominant concepts—society, relations of production, mode of production—do not preclude a broader concept that encompasses them. Clearly, the urban context (the city and its relation to the countryside) is not indifferent to the "degree of civilization."

Following the order indicated above, we can now examine the functions and structures of urban form, bequeathed by history to bourgeois society.

(a) *From the point of view of the formation of surplus value.* The city has no essential function. In effect, the place of exploitation, where surplus value is initially formed, is the unit of production: the enterprise, "society" in the capitalist sense, the branch of industry, as well as large and midsize agricultural production units (employing salaried labor).

In this way, the city, a historical product, supplies what we have called the background of bourgeois society. Rarely does Marx invoke his concept, present it as such; generally, he refers to an English city such as London or Manchester (356ff.). Yet, the city as such remains a productive force for Marx. It contains a significant amount of past and fixed labor, literally dead, which the capitalist uses to capture living labor; what it contains thus survives the daily wear and tear of the instruments of labor (293). Like an institution, it maintains the division of labor essential to the functioning of capitalism and, therefore, it maintains and improves within itself the social division of labor; it brings together the elements of the production process.

CAPITAL AND LAND OWNERSHIP

Here, the role of the city within the forces of production, under capitalism, extends much further than a superficial investigation would assume. Economists since Marx, and even recently, have brought to light the functions of urban reality that concentrate, in space and time, the various aspects of production: enterprises, markets, information and decisions, and so on. These inductive or multiplying effects have less importance, according to Marx, than a much deeper effect. Capitalist society *tends to separate its own conditions from each other*. The effect of separation is inherent to this society, to its efficiency; it is based, practically, on the division of labor pushed to the extreme by the analytic intellect. By projecting them onto the background, by making them perceptible, the separation reveals the internal contradictions of society that are generally inaccessible to the senses. When it separates elements of the population, this segregation can have advantages for capitalism; once it escapes certain limitations, the operation of dissociation has certain drawbacks. What we call an "economic crisis" consists of a *dissociation* of the factors of production: money and commodities (the circuit is broken because commodities no longer realize their exchange value, together with the incorporated surplus value, on the market), use value and exchange value, dead labor (capital) and living labor (labor power), and so on. Fundamentally, at the very foundation of capitalism, we find a separation of the producer (laborer) from the means of production, as well as the initial breakdown of exchange into two separate actions: production and sale (payment in currency). This leads to the separation of the process of production and the process of circulation, "which become exclusive of each other and come into conflict." After the crisis, which is a temporary solution for existing contradictions, the disturbed order is restored. Bourgeois society has been purged of its excess—capital, means of production. The unity of the process, together with the possibility of expanded reproduction, is restored. A good war serves the same function. But the urban context and the city itself act permanently against the dislocation and dissociation in space and time of the conditions of the process; the context implies and contains cohesive forces, even though anticohesive forces are at work as well.

The city contains the population required by the productive apparatus along with the "reserve army" that the bourgeoisie requires to inflect wages and maintain access to a labor "pool." A market of commodities and money (capital), the city also becomes the work market (labor). Once the capitalist regime has taken over agriculture, the demand for labor decreases as capital is accumulated. "Some of the rural population, therefore, finds itself always on the point of being converted into an urban population." *Latent overpopulation,* in the countryside as well as in the city, is one of the phenomena characteristic of capitalism. In the countryside, this excess population is freed by technical progress and the investment of capital in agricultural production; in the city, it is left to drift, depending on the needs of industry, operated by capitalists and managed according to their requirements. Is it necessary to state that the phenomenon analyzed by Marx (*Capital,* vol. 1, chapter 25) has now become *ubiquitous*? There is an excess (latent) of workers and wealth (in spite of wars), for the massive process separates people from wealth.

The productive forces of industry, which tend to be concentrated in cities, act powerfully on rural areas. Large-scale industry has caused a genuine revolution in agriculture and in the social relations of the agents of agricultural production; there has been an increase in the amount of land cultivated but a decrease (relative and absolute) in the rural population and overall depopulation of the countryside. "In the sphere of agriculture, large-scale industry has a more revolutionary effect than elsewhere, for the reason that it annihilates the bulwark of the old society, the 'peasant', and substitutes for him the wage-laborer. Thus the need for social transformation, and the antagonism of the classes, reaches the same level in the countryside as it has attained in the towns" (ibid., 637). The capitalist mode of production replaces the routine exploitation of the land through the technological application

of science. With the increasing importance of the urban population, consolidated in and around large cities, capitalist production accumulates forces capable of acting toward the transformation of society. At the same time, it destroys the physical health
of urban workers and the equilibrium of rural workers; worse, it
disturbs the organic exchanges between man and nature. "By destroying the circumstances surrounding that metabolism, which
originated in a merely natural and spontaneous fashion, it com-
pels its systematic restoration as a regulative law of social production, and in a form adequate to the full development of the
human race" (637–38). In modern agriculture, just as in the industry of cities, "the increase in the productivity and the mobility of labor is purchased at the cost of laying waste and debilitat-
ing labor power itself" (638). Capitalist production, by using the
technology and organization of labor, exhausts the sources from
which wealth springs: the soil and the labor force. But the conditions for a radical change are established (*Capital,* vol. 1, 21, and
Œuvres choisies, vol 2, 113–19).

While the dissemination of agricultural workers broke the
strength of their resistance, concentration increased that of urban
laborers.

During this transformation, the city continued to play an essential role, although it was not a driving force. And that role
meant contributing to the growth of productive forces, the productivity of labor, and the use of technology. Conversely, the combination of technology and the organization of labor during production contributed to the growth of the urban population and
the importance of cities. This was accompanied by the loss of
rural areas, primarily through the industrialization of agricultural
production and the disappearance of the peasantry (and therefore, the village), and the devastation of the land and the destruction of nature.

The complete urbanization of society, which had not only been
anticipated but had gotten under way prior to the development of
capitalism (the reversal of the earlier situation became part of the

basis of the new society, bourgeois society), continued and even accelerated with the domination of large-scale industry, the bourgeoisie, and capital. It is a revolutionary process because it transforms both the surface of the globe and society. Yet, this process wasn't carried out coherently within the framework of capitalist modes of production; it has a negative side, which pushes it forward but tends toward destruction and self-destruction. Capitalism destroys nature and ruins its own conditions, preparing and announcing its revolutionary disappearance. Only later will the exchanges (organic as well as economic) between the social and the natural, the acquired and the spontaneous, be able to reestablish themselves "in a form adequate to the full development of the human race" (*Capital,* vol. 1, 638).

The city, therefore, to the extent that it is bound to productive forces (and consequently to the formation of surplus value), is the seat of this vast contradictory process. It absorbs the countryside and contributes to the destruction of nature; it also destroys its own conditions of existence and must "reestablish them systematically." Although the city, as such, is not external to productive forces nor indifferent to social relations in bourgeois society, it is in the realization of surplus value that it moves to center stage (economically speaking).

(b) *From the point of view of the realization of surplus value.* This realization demands a market first of all and, then, a particular system of credit, discounting, and funds transfer, which enable money (currency) to carry out its function to the fullest extent: the adjustment of exchange values, the circulation of commodities, methods of payment.

It is clear that the extension of the market is associated with that of urban phenomena. No doubt trade facilitated the formation of the medieval town, but it acted in such a way that it stimulated growth throughout the world. Even if the countryside around the town retained its small, local markets or if, conversely, the town scattered "commercial centers" throughout its territory, exchange was concentrated in the towns. The town sheltered the banking system, established in the Middle Ages to sustain currency operations. With the banks and the banking system, an artifice intended to harmonize and balance payments, the monetary system developed into a credit system. This dispensed with actual payments and replaced them with promissory notes, with "fiduciary" or "scriptural" money, which requires confidence. We find that economic crises are followed by monetary crises. At such times, currency no longer operates in its ideal form (scriptural), we demand hard cash. The presumptuous economist and the arrogant bourgeois claimed, and continue to do so, that gold and silver are mere illusions. But here the illusion becomes reality by separating itself from appearance. Liquidity is required, without which commodities stagnate and rot in warehouses and on docks. What, then, is the city? The theater of these dramas, bourgeois dramas, whose echoes are felt among various segments of the population, destined for unemployment because "rich men have no more money."

In this way, and in this way alone, at this stage of development, and within this "artificial" framework and this "artificial" system, as far from nature as possible, money, and everything it carries with it (capital and the power of capitalists), dominates merchandise, its condition, its antecedent, the world in which it is born, from which it profits, and which it maintains. Money becomes the "social matter of wealth" by maximizing its separation from use value and real materials.

This analysis of the urban population is not yet complete. Marx knows that large-scale industry alone is not enough. In fact, he says, its sphere may even be limited and might not cover all aspects of social production (which it nonetheless dominates). Around the large-scale industrial enterprise, and dependent on it, a crowd of small enterprises cling. Some are artisanal in nature, others manufacturers, and others are small or midsize industrial concerns. They perform repairs, maintenance, provide spare parts, finishing operations, and so on. A smattering, a ring of subordinate enterprises generally surrounds a large unit, which drags behind it every period of productive activity. Likewise, in the countryside, a large domain, whether aristocratic or capitalist, wears its crown of poor peasants, agricultural laborers cultivating a small plot for their own needs, and the inevitable small farmers, most often established on mediocre land. The consolidation of these dependent enterprises has its advantages. Moreover, if they establish themselves far from an urban agglomeration, they contribute to the absorption of the countryside by the town. Turned into satellites by large-scale industry, they nevertheless cannot escape the division of labor or capitalism itself.

Finally, and especially, "services" are concentrated in the town and the urban agglomeration. Here we encounter three difficulties, three theoretical discussions that are already well established. First, what do these well-known "services" consist of and how are they defined? Marxist dogmatists, especially politicians anxious to shape their clientele, seek criteria. The "worker" must be a manual laborer, according to some; for others, he must contribute to the creation of surplus value. This leads to endless arguments and hairsplitting, even though the problem (that of the *class* retaining unity in spite of the particularities of its factions) is not a false problem. Do transport workers, bank employees, and merchants directly produce surplus value, even though they do not produce "things," commodities? Do they contribute indirectly to surplus value because of the fact that they intervene in the circulation of commodities, which is essential to the realization of surplus value? Are they remunerated on the basis of overall surplus value?

This is an old, truly byzantine discussion that I don't want to take up here (the apprentice hairdresser would produce surplus value, whereas the owner would receive a share of the overall surplus value, and so on). What is important is that Marx distinguishes *productive labor* (of things, of commodities) and *unproductive but socially necessary labor* (for example, that of a scholar or educator, or a teacher in general, or a physician, and so on). Moreover, for Marx, if all productive workers are salaried, all salaried workers are not immediately and directly productive (of things, of exchangeable goods). As for the term "service," it is merely an expression to refer to a *use value,* provided in exchange for a sum of money by an "agent" who may possess his own means of production; he provides a "service" as an activity, this service being bought and sold like a thing even though it is not necessarily a thing. Material labor can be purchased as a "service," for example, that of a skilled worker who repairs a water pipe or gas conduit. The same type of activity can be considered productive or unproductive labor. The poet creates poetry, says Marx, just as the silkworm creates silk, because that is his nature; but once that poetry is published, it produces surplus value by and for the publisher and the bookseller; it supplies productive labor to the printer, and so on.[5]

The polemic is a long-standing one. Marx rejected the "productivism" of Adam Smith, the great economist, theoretician, and "classic" thinker of bourgeois society but a man incapable of criticizing political economy and his own economism. Smith dreamed (a utopian dream but one that was "positive" for Smith) of a society composed of producers and producers alone, supplying the maximum of things, the maximum productive social labor, and, consequently, surplus value (although Smith did not identify or formulate the concept). Marx, much more open-minded than the puritan and moralist Smith because he maintained a critical position toward economics and economism, did not dismiss as "parasitic" the various "services" provided. Moreover, it is interesting, and somewhat paradoxical, that the labor movement and "proletarian" politics have frequently made use of the position of the bourgeois economist in opposition to Marx's ideas. Economism, productivism, and moralism all have their needs.

Here we again encounter the question "What does it mean to produce?" in the broadest sense of the term: to produce knowledge, works, gaiety, pleasure, not only things or objects, exchangeable material goods. Marx had always rejected *reductivism* and the tendencies toward reductive thinking he observed around him, especially among economists. But almost no one followed him along these lines, much less understood him.

Now we can ask a second question, "What is a society?" As mentioned earlier, large-scale industry, for Marx, creates a working class but not a society. No more than "production" in the narrow sense does. For there to be a "society," a wide variety of people and activities are needed. In the *Critique of the Gotha Program* (1875), Marx harshly reminded the leaders of the labor movement, already established behind a mix of economism and political statism, of this fact. A society requires artists, professional entertainers. Are there parasites? Certainly. The speculators who insist that their money must "work" for them and make money directly, for example. Nor can we easily identify a clear demarcation between those who are unproductive but socially necessary and social parasites. Who today is unfamiliar with Marx's ironic fragment in which he celebrates the criminal: "A philosopher produces ideas, a poet poems. . . . A criminal produces crimes. If we take a closer look at the connection between this latter branch of production and society as a whole, we shall rid ourselves of many prejudices."[6] What does the criminal produce? The law, the police, justice, morality, crime novels, the sentiment of tragedy, and so on. In short, he interrupts the day-to-day monotony and security of bourgeois life. He protects it against stagnation and generates an uneasy tension, the mobility without which the incentive for competition would be damped. He also provides a spur to productive forces.[7]

The city contains everything that we have enumerated and analyzed: excess populations, satellites of large-scale industry, "services" of every kind (from the best to the worst), as well as an administrative and political apparatus, bureaucrats and managers, the bourgeoisie and its followers. In this way the city and society move together, blend together, because the city incorporates, as "capital," capitalist power itself, the state. It is within this framework that the distribution of the resources of society takes place, a prodigious mix of sordid calculation and senseless waste.

However, before looking at things from this point of view (the distribution of surplus value), we encounter the problems raised by Rosa Luxemburg. Although this problem postdates Marx and the analysis found in *Capital,* it is largely the result of them and shouldn't be overlooked. More important, we have a response to the problems raised by Luxemburg, which can be found, although not yet clearly formulated, in the arguments and works set forth by Marx and presented so far.

In *The Accumulation of Capital,* Luxemburg points out a weakness in Marxist theory and the section of *Capital* devoted to the realization of surplus value.[8] Laborers who work in an industry can only purchase a share of the products produced, those that correspond to their salary. Yet, on the basis of Marxist theory, this share is minimal because the difference between the sum of all salaries and the total value of those products constitutes surplus value itself. This surplus value can only be realized in a market that is external to capitalist society. Surplus value is realized and can only be realized among peasants and nonindustrialized peoples, for whom such transactions inevitably end in ruin. This leads to the no less inevitable collapse of capitalism following a decisive crisis. The far limits of industrial capitalism, markets in which its products are sold, are eaten away by capitalism; it destroys itself in the process of destroying its conditions. Marx had predicted this, but not exactly in the way that Luxemburg understood.

Lenin replied that capitalists obtain, within capitalism, a significant and sufficient portion of surplus value because of the fact that large-scale industry (section I on production, in *Capital*) is primarily involved in producing the *means of production*: machinery and raw materials. These products of large-scale capitalist industry are bought and paid for by other capitalists. There follows an increase in the productive forces, for these capitalists invest their available capital in production. The overproduction inherent in this process appears as a depression or cyclical crisis (rather than a final crisis, as Luxemburg predicted).

We can now complete Lenin's argument. Arranged around the

seeds of large-scale industrial production and bureaucratic power, we find, in the modern city, very diverse layers of workers, employees, and professions. These layers are not part of the polarization between "the proletariat and large-scale industry." However, they are not outside capitalism, either with respect to production or with respect to the market and consumption. Nor do they coincide with the definition of the industrial proletariat or that of manual or immediately productive labor. Although large-scale industry (sector 1) can distribute a large percentage of its products in a capitalist milieu, although it seeks outside markets for the remainder, a considerable portion of the goods produced in sector 2 (production of consumable goods) flows into the urban milieu, which extends far beyond the working class strictly speaking. In a society dominated and managed by the bourgeoisie, the market is not reduced to the proletariat. There is an internal market, and the strategy of capitalist managers has been at work (for several decades) trying to expand it. The recourse to external markets is certainly essential and stimulating, but not as Luxemburg believed, not as an absolute necessity. Otherwise the growth of productive forces under capitalism would be incomprehensible.[9]

And yet, isn't Luxemburg largely correct with respect to Lenin's arguments? The economic and political centers of capitalist society want to make sure that products are distributed and surplus value realized. Not only do they manipulate the market (through advertising), they protect it (through customs tariffs and price stabilization); they control it. The reproduction of surplus value and the social relations of production can no longer be separated—not without new contradictions. As social space is produced, it is monitored and controlled together with the growth of large cities and the development of national territory. Therefore, if the bourgeoisie of such an industrial country loses its external markets, it brings colonialism home, to the interior of the country. The peripheries, in comparison to the centers (of economic production and political decision making), give rise to the phenomena of neocolonialism and neo-imperialism. The

social layers juxtaposed in the urban space include few peasants
but a number of populations that are dispersed and dominated by
the centers. The modern city (metropolis, megalopolis) is, at the
same time, the seat, instrument, and center of activity of neocolonialism and neo-imperialism.[10]

How can we explain, using Marx's terms, this body of facts,
which he had not anticipated and could not anticipate? Returning
to Marx after the critical interpretations of Luxemburg and Lenin,
I now want to examine the importance of land and ground rent.

(c) *In terms of the distribution of surplus value.* This distribution moves through the highest level of capitalist society, namely,
the most general, which is to say national, even international (to
the extent that there is an international market, competition of
capital on the international market, and so on). It takes place on
the economic and political levels. Economically, every capitalist
receives a share of surplus value, proportional (approximately) to
the amount of capital employed by him. A general average is realized, namely, the average rate of profit, which depends on several variables, primarily the average organic composition of capital. In his language, the capitalist calculates his production costs,
his depreciation, profits, dividends to be paid out to lenders, future investments; his accounting is based on what is, for him, a
solid foundation of empiricism and a corresponding logic. Marxist thought looks at the same data differently, using another language and different concepts: constant capital (investments and
dead labor), variable capital (wages, capital put into circulation by
labor), the organic composition of capital, surplus product, surplus value, average rate of profit. The two languages, the two different "accountings," are comparable, but the second explains the
first by dissipating the illusions of capitalism and the appearances
of bourgeois society.

Politically, the state takes a portion of the surplus value to pay
the general expenses of bourgeois society, which no individual
capitalist is likely to assume. How does this work? Taking extreme
care to secure the interests of the managerial class, it "imposes"

taxation. The taxation and fee system is conducted in several ways; for example, through state monopolies and the sale of commodities intended to satisfy "needs" whose social character cannot always be guaranteed (salt, tobacco, matches, documents bearing the state seal, and so on).[11] In the forefront, we have the *maintenance of state bureaucracy* (which reproduces itself while ensuring the re-production of its own conditions, which tends to ensure the re-production of the relations of production throughout society and in the mode of production). The state has its own interests, through which it tends, especially in France and in the West generally, to erect itself on top of society, to establish itself by masking the contradictions of that society, crushing them through repression or concealing them behind clouds of ideology. It promotes a "state reason" that is, ideologically, confused with reason in general. Similarly, through bureaucracy the state maintains a repressive apparatus: the army, police, legal system, and so on.

But the state must also administer and concern itself with *social needs,* those of society as a whole. The list of those needs and their interconnections have never been established and cannot be established. Politically, it's a matter of relations of force; but in this sense (otherwise significant), the democratic (bourgeois or not) state remains sensitive and vulnerable to pressure from below, to demands. Its contractual system cannot become static. New needs—social and individual needs—appear, initially the needs of workers as such but also those of large subgroups: women, children, the sick and the elderly, delinquents, the insane.

We return to these aspects of modern society because we should expect to very quickly see the needs of urban life, of the *city,* become such "social needs." Considered as a social unit, the site of (social) relations between men ("culture") and nature, throughout history the city seems to be among the beneficiaries of the political distribution of global surplus product (surplus value) by the state. *But this is not the case.* We have to wait until the twentieth century, and the second half of the twentieth century at that, for concepts such as urbanism, "community facilities," land-use planning, and so on to emerge. Beneath their "objective" appearance, these were vague, even tendentious; images and metaphors more than concepts.

When Marx, in the *Critique of the Gotha Program,* lists the social needs that a socialist state must consider, what does he include? General administrative expenses that don't affect production (expenses intended to decline, then disappear in a transformed society), schools, public health (factors intended to increase considerably), funds for those who are no longer able to work (what, in official language today, is known as public assistance).[12] No doubt urban needs are part of "public health," a rather summary designation.

This absence is even more remarkable given that the concept of the rational organization of production (planning) intended to satisfy developing "social needs" is constantly appearing in Marx; *it defines socialism.* For Marx, the rational organization of production includes organic exchanges between society and nature, exchanges of raw materials and energy that support the exchange of material goods within society. Yet, our author knows that given capitalism's relentless exploitation of all sources of wealth, nature itself is threatened. The regulation of organic exchanges must become a "governing law" of the new society. How can this result be obtained without fully accounting for the city itself, the site of those exchanges, the milieu and seat of permanent aggression against nature?

Nothing better demonstrates this than the fact that in a regime (system or mode of production) in which the economic is dominant and where the state controls this primacy, historical and social relations are subordinate to the imperatives of the economic. Concern for large-scale industrial corporations takes precedence over all others. And what about the city? Its influence on production and productivity, on the exchange of goods, is taken into account, ensured, controlled on behalf of a general control over social space. In itself it is merely an object of use bequeathed by the past, now become an object of exchange and consumption the same as any other negotiable "thing." It is not privileged; it attracts no special attention. Until the day when something new arrives, which overturns the trivial calculus of profitability.

Such neglect of "social needs" at some point raises the possibility of an accumulation that would see itself as a goal, as an end. Social needs would be provided but kept to a strict minimum. The maximum (possible) social surplus product would go toward investment and, consequently, to "uses" of those productive investments that facilitate accumulation and the anticipation of further investment—in particular, the military and armaments. From this perspective, economics and political economy would function autonomously, whereby production directly and immediately ensured the (expanded) re-production of products as well as the re-production of the conditions (relations) of production. We might even wonder whether the tendency toward the autonomization of production and *economic* conditions isn't essential in modern societies, but concealed by the apparent autonomy of technology (justifying itself in this way) and legitimized by the increase in population. Such autonomization of the economic would occur to the extent that *democratic* pressure fails to bring *social needs* to the foreground, massively, from the base. It also provides an estimate of the significance of this pressure "at the base" and, consequently, demands upon the city.

Once the state comes into being, extra-economic constraints and pressures, exercised by the state apparatus, produce economic effects. Conversely, economic interactions give rise to extra-economic pressures that complement them. This state pressure is such that it determines, for as long as states have existed, the *surplus labor* (the portion of products that exceeds immediate, individual, and social needs) and, consequently, the *overall surplus value* in so-called capitalist society. The state's political and strategic goals, especially the resources allocated to war (the armed forces, armaments), are not the result of the use of preexisting surplus labor (surplus value) but *impose* a redistribution of resources. That is why critical analysis of these proportions incorporates all the elements of a fundamental challenge.

Under these conditions, we might wonder whether the city has not been, ever since the state came into being, the "accursed share" of society, in the sense that Georges Bataille gave to the term: the share of sacrifice, that is, the share that is sacrificed and the share for which we must make sacrifices from time to time.[13] But this idea is still far too attractive. The accursed share was that of warfare and festivals and erotic passion. During the bourgeois era, the festival disappeared or became a profitable undertaking: commercial fairs, fairs underwritten for reasons that had nothing to do with the joy of the festival itself. The festival was "co-opted" or forbidden. Armaments allow for the realization of surplus value at the same time as they supply the means of repression. War beneficially replaces an economic crisis of overproduction, liquidates any surplus, and leads to a new beginning that is proportional to the destruction caused (and strangely favors the destroyed nations).

We could make use of the concept of *civilization*, found scattered throughout Marx's work as distinct from the *mode of production*. Marx did not provide a methodical development of the concept but Nietzsche did. It could easily be shown, using urban reality as an illustration and principal argument, that bourgeois society during its key periods—rise, growth, prosperity—presents and represents no more than a "crisis of civilization."

These considerations, however, could not be considered part of what Marx, at least, felt to be essential. The difficulties arise primarily because of *landed property*, that of the soil, and the rents that are based on it.

The liberal (bourgeois) radicalism of the Belle Époque hoped to break these historically determined chains through the growth and development of society. It hoped to eliminate (private) landed property, arable or not. This radicalism was intent on destroying the old class of landed property owners through political action. These ambitions, these grand political goals, were unsuccessful.

The French Revolution itself settled for "agrarian reform." It was the first and one of the most extensive but limited to a transfer of ownership (confiscation of the assets of emigrants, purchase of those assets by the rising bourgeoisie).

Ownership of the land was seen as part of private property in general. Although this landed property had been superseded by movable assets—money and capital—it persisted. In fact, it grew stronger for, ever since Marx, the bourgeoisie grew richer by purchasing land and creating landed properties (and, consequently, reconstituting landed property and ground rent) through new monopolies. Ownership of the land, ultimately intact and reconstituted by capitalism, *was a weight that dragged down all of society.*

The umbilical cord that tied society to nature was badly severed. What did the cut require and what did the break imply? The city. The connection had dried up but the vital exchange between the community and the earth was not replaced by rational regulation, yet society remained attached, even bound, to the soil through ownership and the multiple forms of servitude it supported. This occurred primarily by subordinating the soil to *the market* and making the earth a marketable "good" associated with exchange value and speculation rather than use and use value. The umbilical cord, which fed sap and blood from the womb of origin to its progeny, the human community, became a rope, a hard, dry cord, which hobbled the movement and development of that community. It was the ultimate restraint.

It is important to note that, since Marx, no satisfactory solution has eliminated the problem by surpassing the facts and conditions of its existence. State ownership of the land transfers to the state a significant portion of ground rent ("absolute" rent, according to Marx, as well as a portion of the differential rent that arises from the increased value of agricultural products in the vicinity of markets, that is to say, cities). This transfer would assign to the state tremendous resources and power, while leaving the peasants with legally and contractually limited "enjoyment," or usufruct, of the soil. This is not what Marx intended when he defined socialism. And as far as nationalization and municipalization of the land are concerned, we are more familiar with their limitations and drawbacks than we are with their advantages.

The question of ground rent appears to be a thing of the past, yet it retains its importance. It has even grown in importance because buildable land in the industrial city, its price, and the speculation associated with it are part of theory but seemingly marginal when compared to the theory of profit and wages. "Wherever rent exists at all, differential rent appears at all times and is governed by the same laws, as agricultural differential rent. Wherever natural forces can be monopolized and guarantee a surplus profit to the industrial capitalist using them, be it waterfalls, rich mines, waters teeming with fish, or a favorably located building site, there the person who by virtue of title to a portion of the globe has become the proprietor of these natural objects will wrest this surplus profit from functioning capital in the form of rent."[14] With respect to buildable land, Adam Smith has shown that its rent, like that of all nonagricultural land, is based on agricultural rent, strictly speaking, that is, on the rent of location and the rent of equipment, which correspond to Marx's differential rents I and II. The influence of location is especially important in the large cities.[15] Thus, some precapitalist traits penetrate capitalism. They not only accentuate its agricultural sphere but enter its very core, urban reality. There, they exercise a profound influence, mostly by pulling it toward the past. Of course, capitalists take back from the owner of the land the largest possible amount of rent that he has withdrawn from them, which also happens to result in the "complete passivity" of this owner, whose entire activity consists in taking advantage of the progress to which he contributes nothing and for which he risks nothing, unlike the industrial capitalist. When the industrial capitalist takes ownership of the soil and landed property, when it is concentrated in the same hands as capital, then capitalists hold such great power that they can even expel struggling workers "from the earth as a dwelling place."

(a) *Quantitatively.* Ground rents, among which we should include those that arise from agricultural production, pasturing, hunting, fishing, the use of streams and forests, mining (when the subsoil does not belong to the state), and finally rents from buildings (the built domain), have all undergone fluctuations.

In France, the democratic (bourgeois, yes, but quite advanced) revolution and correlative agrarian reform attenuated for nearly a century the disadvantages of landed property in the countryside and the importance of landowners. Their impact was greater in the countryside than the city, for speculation in land, as well as military concerns, had guided the transformation of Paris by Baron Haussmann. During the twentieth century, land ownership was reconstituted under capitalism, industrialization took over agricultural production, especially for large-scale crop production (wheat, beets), specialized crops (vineyards, market gardens, milk), and pasturing. The former feudal monopoly gave way to the new capitalist monopoly; in some regions these coexisted or cooperated through alliances. Under these conditions, land ownership regained the influence it appeared to have lost. This was felt in several ways. The land and even space itself were sold in parcels. The exchangeability of space becomes increasingly important in the transformation of cities. Even architecture is dependent on this, for the form of buildings is determined by lot size and the purchased land that is broken up into small rectangles. The housing sector becomes, belatedly but increasingly obviously, a sector subordinate to large-scale capitalism, occupied by corporations (industrial, commercial, banking), whose profitability is carefully managed under cover of land-use planning. The process that subordinated productive forces to capitalism was here reproduced through the subordination of space that had been put on the market for capital investment, that is, both for profit and for the reproduction of the relations of capitalist production. The profits were immense and the (underlying) law of the decline of the average rate of profit was quite effectively contradicted. On the one hand, land rent (rent I provided by the best land closest to urban markets, and rent II, technical rent obtained from the investment of capital in agricultural production) continued to increase, to the benefit of capitalists, along with the growth of cities. Additionally, within that urban expansion, certain types of income reappear, primarily agricultural ground rents such as pure economic income and capital investment income, which are difficult to quantify.

Outside France, the importance of landed property has never disappeared, except in countries that engaged in agrarian reform. Immense continents such as America and Africa have hardly been touched by this revolutionary reform. The great domains (the "latifundia") exercise an influence that contributes greatly to the political chaos in which a number of countries find themselves immersed.

Here I would like to briefly comment on the theory of land occupation and population concentration described by Marx and Lenin. Lenin, developing some of Marx's ideas, identified and contrasted two methods of colonization (in the broad sense, the installation of "colonists," farmers, and agricultural production units). These are limit cases, poles between which any number of actual or possible situations fall. The Prussian method consists in the sudden colonization of previously appropriated (possessed) lands; those who direct the operation are already landowners, country squires, feudal lords. They employ violence and operate in stages, and the colonists remain their vassals. The American way of colonization is entirely different. In this case, free colonists settle on free land (an abstraction that ignores the indigenous populations, who, generally, do not practice permaculture, with permanent villages and towns). Occupation of the land and the installation of large agricultural production units do not encounter obstacles from an older and well-established society or mode of production, as was the case with medieval society in Europe. These free colonists come from previously existing cities that contain markets and trading centers, and are often on the path to industrialization. American capitalism did not have to overturn or destroy an earlier society; it expanded without obstacles and without any resistance other than that from the indigenous populations. The rural background, so powerful in Europe, was missing, and this lack became an obsession, culturally speaking. It has a heightened urban character but the city, in its unrestricted expansion across the countryside, achieved no sense of self-assurance, no self-awareness. In this extra-historical context, appreciably different from historical development in the Far East and Western Europe, the city established its hold over rural territories. But today, the situation has been reversed: the city, even the largest, is becoming ruralized, rather than urbanizing its "environment."

Also, although landed property didn't exist in the United States as something that predated capitalism, it became securely established through it. After two centuries, its pressure and extent are hardly less than they are in old Europe. And Europe has been the victim of social and political forces it has been unable to eliminate: feudal forces in Prussia (the Junkers), the latifundia in Spain, and so on.

Quantitatively, therefore, throughout the world, the pressure of land ownership remains considerable, both for agricultural production and for the process of urbanization. This influence is poorly understood and the numbers that would help us evaluate it are often hidden from view.[16] Marx asks how the landowner, without access to capital, without investing, can capture a portion of surplus value. He replies that the formal nature of property (the rights of ownership) allows this. Without even exploiting the land, without touching it with his fingers, even absent, he can extract from it the so-called absolute rent and a large portion of the so-called differential rent arising from the variation in the land, its variable fertility, more or less favorable location, work carried out, and capital invested. This is initially possible only because agriculture as a whole is a retrograde sector of capitalist production; the organic composition of capital (investments) is smaller here than elsewhere and, consequently, the role of living labor (the number of workers) is greater. It is from this living labor that the owner withdraws, either directly or through an intermediary, his "revenue," that is, his share of global surplus value.

Clearly, this explanation satisfies the analysis only with respect to landed property of the traditional kind: feudal in origin and consisting of large domains contracted out to farmers or summarily exploited as grazing land. It has to be modified for mines and advanced agriculture. With respect to the "built domain," it is applicable to the ancient proprietor, who, through an "entrepreneur," could have a building constructed that could then be rented out. This is no longer applicable to modern construction and the subsequent involvement of large, well-equipped companies, banks, and various agencies. However, these phenomena are recent, especially in France. The "real-estate" sector has been mobilized slowly, that is, subjected to capitalism; moreover, the process is far from complete. It is in this context of heightened industrialization that we again find "urban rents" that are related to rural ground rents: pure economic income (differential rent I) and capital investment income (rent II). To this should be added absolute rent, which every owner claims by the very fact of ownership and which is used as the basis for speculation. This means that "real-estate" theory (with its characteristic features: ground rent and the commercialization of space, capital investment and the opportunity for profit), for a long time a secondary sector and only gradually integrated into capitalism, is still being developed. This (critical) theory specifically covers the process of integration, the subordination to capitalism of a sector that was long outside it, together with the integration of agriculture in its entirety (except for the "peripheries") with industry and capitalism.

Marx's texts on landed capitalism and rent culminate in this theory, which they do not contain but to which they allude and describe (vol. 3, book 8). However, the symbolic role of landed property greatly exceeds its "real" economic (quantitative) effects.

(b) *Qualitatively.* Landed property pulls all of society backward; not only does it slow growth and paralyze development, it uses constant pressure to orient their development. Shouldn't the hybrid character of urban expansion be attributed to this imperceptible but perpetual activity? Suburban areas, half-town, half-country (that is, neither town nor country), arise from this pressure. The owner of a plot of land imagines himself to be a rural landowner, the owner of a fragment of nature. But he is neither peasant nor citizen. Urbanization extends to the countryside but is degraded and degrading. Rather than the city absorbing and reducing the countryside, we have a kind of reciprocal degradation: the city explodes into outlying areas and the village deteriorates; an uncertain urban fabric proliferates throughout the entire country. A shapeless magma is the result: slums and metastasized cities. In terms taken from Marx, the ruralization of the city is a threat, substituting itself for the urbanization of the countryside, a phenomenon that mirrors the decline of ancient cities. This transpires in spite of the power of industry and beneath the uneasy, but complicit, gaze of the representatives of the managerial class, who find substantial profit in this breakdown. Warnings and criticisms go unheeded for the most part. Possession has not grown destitute; it has not given up its place, not even its prestige. The practical and ideological pressure of private property (the land together with capital) *blinds* the managers, even the intellectuals; it obsesses the imagination of architects and urbanists. This blindness arises from two sources: the images deriving directly or indirectly from possession and those deriving from the rationality of business (technical division of labor). The urban remains an abstraction, an elsewhere, a utopia. And the rural, ruined and soiled, invades all of society. A ruined nature collapses at the feet of this superficially satisfied society. Such behavior cannot be separated from other aspects of a theoretical and practical situation whose paradoxes dissimulate its contradictions.

During his last years, in his writings Marx circled closer and closer to the concept of mode of production. For him, defining the capitalist mode of production did not mean constructing a "model," as was subsequently claimed, nor did it mean systematizing his concept of society in general and bourgeois society in particular. Instead of closing down reality, instead of "enclosing" the concept, he opened it up. Neither the past nor the future of the capitalist mode of production was closed off. In the future, large-scale industry would lead or push, a half-blind, half-known (or misunderstood) force. The past drags land ownership along with it, prolonging all that came before. Marx never held the view, which has since been attributed to him, of a capitalist mode of production that would encompass several modes of production, one of which—capitalism—would be dominant or "overdetermining" and thereby allow political entities to "structure" and impose, through the system of power, a coherence on other systems: economic, ideological, and so on.

It's true that Marx, for many years, found himself confronting a new "problematic," which he formulated without providing any resolution. Did his inability to complete *Capital* arise from this? No doubt. However, it cannot be explained solely by Marx's illness or the extent or alteration of his immediate concerns; the increasing number of new—and unresolved—questions must also be taken into consideration.

With the failure of the commune and the rise of a large-scale workers' movement that did not follow the path outlined by Marx, capitalism grew stronger. This was something Marx never completely excluded, even though the growth of productive forces under capitalism had surprised him. This implies that the *relations of production are reproduced*. During an earlier period, Marx foresaw this phenomenon, especially in the *Grundrisse*. But the immediately given phenomenon was the simple or expanded reproduction of the labor force, of the means of production. Wages should allow the working class to reproduce itself, and the proletariat to have and raise children, until the moment they themselves become part of the production process. Around 1875 the problem changed. How did it come about that after one or more generations, and with the changes in society, the relations of production were still held to be essential? It was no longer a question of economic cycles or the expanded reproduction of the means of production, but of a different social phenomenon. Marx did not discuss the structural cohesion or the imminent dislocation of the mode of production. He explored neither a "subject" nor a "system," but a *process*. And during this process, contradictions were also produced, reproduced, became attenuated or grew more profound, appeared or disappeared. For the process as a whole is accompanied by the *expanded reproduction of contradictions* (old and new).

Analysis of the process reveals subjects (agents or actors: groups, classes, and subclasses) but not a Subject. It is a product of partial systems (for example, the contract or quasi-contract system in a given society, within the mode of production) but not a System. The mode of production is defined by all of these interactions.

The contradiction between the productive forces and (capitalist) relations of production is only one conflictual relation among many; essential, yes, but variable in its intensity and influence. Wouldn't the "overdetermining" contradiction, if we accept this terminology, consist in the permanent conflict between the effort to ensure the consistency of the social whole and the perpetual rebirth of contradictions in every domain? This contradiction creates violence but is resolved only temporarily through repression and constraint. If the domains and sectors are multiplied and diversified when reproduction of the relations of production (including urban reality) is complete, the contradictions as well are multiplied and diversified between and within domains and sectors.

If this is the case, the analysis of "urban" problems under the capitalist mode of production—if we are to extend Marx's work—cannot consist in the discovery or construction of a modern "urban system" or "urban power," but in the disclosure of contradictions typical of urban phenomena considered as part of an overall process. Nor would the simple description of urban chaos or malaise, similar to a phenomenology, be suitable for this method and this orientation. What is needed is an analysis, based on concepts and developing into a theory, that seeks to provide a comprehensive explanation of the process.

I want to close this chapter with a few more words of commentary. The city and urban reality would be, under this hypothesis, the site par excellence and the ensemble of sites in which are carried out cycles of re-production that are larger and more complex than those of production, which they comprise. In particular, the reproduction of (capitalist) relations of production implies the reproduction of the division of labor, that is, a separation within the division of labor and, in particular, between the technical (among the units of production) and social division of labor (the market). It's possible that the city or what remains of it (population centers) might become the site of this reproduction as well as the persistent link between these terms, which tend to break down.

As for the reproduction of knowledge, it incorporates not only the reproduction of social relations (through the relation between teacher and student) but that of ideologies, mixed with concepts and theories, that take the form of topics, citations, whether concealed or revealed, "research," evaluations, redundancies mixed with information, reductions that are more or less contradicted, and so on. A certain relation between knowledge and non-knowledge, which ideology holds together, is also transmitted—especially when it concerns Marxism and the city.

Conclusion

Of course, we haven't exhausted Marx's thinking about the city and if we were to identify all the texts by Marx and Engels in which the word *city* appears, we would make further discoveries, especially concerning class struggle. For both authors this incessant combat had its origin in production, its basis in economic reality, its motives in its demands, its active support in the working class. And yet, the class struggle occurs in the city. The political struggle reflects a political situation yet reveals aspects and latent possibilities of that situation that have gone unnoticed. As it begins to transform the relations of production, the class struggle makes us conscious of them. That is how the relations between "town and country" become perceptible within a specific context. In 1848 French cities and towns rejected the political influence of the then largest class in French society, that of the owners of smallholdings, the peasants. The citizens of the towns succeeded in "falsifying the meaning of the December 10, 1848, election" and delaying the rise of Bonapartism. For the small-holding peasants, Bonaparte had for several years merely "broken the fetters that the towns imposed on the will of the countryside." But the peasant and his holding were the result of the extension to the countryside of the regime of unrestricted competition and large-scale industry, which had its origins in the towns under Napoleon I. During this process, however, the interests of the peasants ceased to harmonize with those of the bourgeoisie, and they would find their ally and guide "in the urban proletariat, whose task is the overthrow of the bourgeois order."[1]

Having said this, looking back, we must consider the path traveled so we can obtain a better perspective of the path that lies before us.

The texts by Marx and Engels on the city have revealed their meaning only by being considered in terms of the movement of their thought as whole. They have forced us to return to that movement, which was lost but has now been found. They cannot be isolated. To examine them separately would mean betraying the movement that carried them forward. That is why it was necessary, for understanding the economic role of the cities, to review the theory of surplus value, the division of labor, and so on.

Some readers may wonder "What exactly are you asking? To discover what Marx and Engels knew and wrote a century ago about a question that was then beginning to be asked, by examining texts that no one has yet thought to reunite? What gives you the right to mix current interests with a review of those texts and their close study?"

Others will exclaim, "But that's not at all what we were expecting! We were hoping that by employing Marx's method, rather than extending his doctrine, a contemporary Marxist would tell us what he knows about questions that are being asked with growing urgency. What use are those texts if they serve no purpose?"

To the first, we again say that, in our opinion, Marxology has little interest. In his name we have embalmed and stuffed various "thinkers" and a way of thinking that remain current, in the sense that we cannot understand the present moment without them and must begin with them if we are to understand what has transpired over the past century. Erudition, the descent into the "historic," is of no interest here. I have examined these texts on behalf of the present and the possible; and that is, precisely, Marx's method, the one he recommended so that the past (events and documents) might live on and serve the future.

To the second we would object that the controversies surrounding Marx's thought prevent the use of concepts without prior examination. To extend Marx's thought to an "object" that he has not explicitly examined, it must first be reformulated. Only then can we make use of the critical analysis of competitive capitalism used by Marx for the modern city and its problematic.

In truth, the author (ego) has considered this reformulation for a long time and attempted to continue these analyses before publishing the results of his rereading. Evidence of this can be seen, if need be, in various—implicitly or explicitly—"Marxist" books and publications.

The search to extend Marx's thought does not attempt to discover or construct consistency: an "urban system," urban structures and functions within the capitalist mode of production. A way of thinking that can properly be called "Marxist" subordinates consistency to contradiction. If we must accept the opposite, namely, the subordination of conflicts to the forces of cohesion in capitalist society, it is because Marx has erred, because his thinking has strayed, and the bourgeoisie has won.

I have sketched some of the problems that have come to light in the second half of the nineteenth century as a result of the critical analysis of the (capitalist) mode of production and how these were addressed by the (bourgeois) managers of that society. These had to consider, in their political practice, the re-production of the relations of production, not only of the means of production. Expanded reproduction affects not only the cycles and circuits of economic production but more complex processes. Those problems, the bourgeoisie—following strategies similar to those implemented by Bismarck—resolved empirically but effectively, effectively enough to maintain the capitalist mode of production. Marxist thought, however, split into "reformism" and "revolutionism": on the one hand, the quest for social logic and, on the other hand, announcement of the catastrophe. Marx, although he anticipated these new problems, was unable to come up with a response.

The re-production of relations of production implies the extension as well as the enlargement of the mode of production and its material base. Capitalism spread to the entire world, incorporating, as Marx had anticipated, earlier productive forces, transforming them for its own purposes. But capitalism also created new sectors of production and, as a result, new sectors of exploitation and domination; among them we find: leisure, daily life, knowledge and art, and, finally, urbanization.

What is the result of this twofold process? Capitalism has sustained itself, extending to all of space. Having begun during Marx's lifetime in a handful of countries (England, a portion of Europe, and North America), it conquered the globe, and successfully created an international market (notably, the creation of leisure activities, tourism, and so on) and in spite of serious setbacks, revolutions, and revolts.

As productive forces grew (in spite of the "limitations" of capitalist relations of production), stimulated by two world wars, they achieved such power that they *produced space*. On the worldwide scale, space is not only discovered and occupied, it is transformed, to the extent that its "raw material," "nature," is threatened by this *domination,* which is not *appropriation*. Generalized *urbanization* is an aspect of this colossal extension. And if space is produced, wouldn't there also be contradictions associated with that space or, more specifically, conflicts imminent in that production, new contradictions? If the answer is yes, then Marx's thought retains his meaning and even assumes greater scope. If not, we must abandon Marx and Marxism. It is pointless to preserve them on the basis of a "scientificity" appropriated by capitalism, whose criteria, moreover, do not apply to them.

It can be demonstrated, however (this "demonstration" is already under way and will be continued elsewhere, in other research and other writings), that the contradictions of space and its production have intensified.

(a) The principal contradiction is found between globally produced space, on a worldwide scale, and the fragmentation and pulverization that result from capitalist relations of production (private ownership of the means of production and the earth, that is, of space itself). Space crumbles, is exchanged (sold) in bits and pieces, investigated piecemeal by the fragmented sciences, whereas it is formed as a worldwide and, even, interplanetary totality.

(b) The extension of capitalism extends Marx's critical analysis of its "trinitarian" constitution. To define this extension as generalized exchange in the "world of commodities" is not enough; it would mean reducing it to the international market alone, which was already in place during Marx's lifetime. The society and the mode of production that define it dissociate and separate their elements while maintaining them in a unity that is imposed and superimposed on that separation. This is the "trinitarian formula" of land, capital, and labor. The capitalist mode of production imposes a repressive (state) unity on the generalized separation (segregation) of groups, functions, and places. And it does this in what is known as urban space.

(c) This space is the seat of a specific contradiction. The city continues to grow without limit; it bursts. As society is urbanized and the countryside absorbed by the city, the city is simultaneously ruralized. Urban extensions (suburbs, the urban periphery) are subject to ownership of the land and its consequences: ground rent, speculation, spontaneous or intentional scarcity.

(d) Mastery over nature, associated with technology and the growth of productive forces, and subject solely to the demands of profit (surplus value), culminates in the destruction of nature. The flow of organic exchange between society and the earth, a flow whose importance Marx pointed out in his discussion of the town, is, if not broken, at least dangerously modified. With the risk of serious, even catastrophic results. We may very well ask whether the destruction of nature is not an "integral" part of society's self-destruction, a turning against itself, while maintaining the capitalist mode of production, its forces, and its power.

(e) No form of the supersession foreseen by the Marxist project is carried out, not that of the "city–country" opposition, not that of the division of labor, and not that of the less well-known opposition between "work and product." This is followed by the reciprocal deterioration of the terms that are not overcome, an especially perceptible and significant degradation with respect to the city and the country.

(f) In contrast to the dispersion to outlying areas, to the segregation that threatens social relations, we encounter a centrality that emphasizes its forms, having become the center of decision making (wealth, information, power, violence).

(g) The production of space does not take time into account unless it is to shackle it to the demands and requirements of productivity. A strange circle in which time is enclosed.

(h) As nonwork is made possible through automation, the managerial bourgeoisie captures this potential for its own use. It extends leisure time only when it can be subordinated to surplus value through the industrialization and commercialization of leisure and leisure spaces. It sterilizes nonwork by monopolizing it for its own indolence, which lacks any creative capacity. It stimulates this symptomatic revolt, the demand for nonwork, which remains marginal (hippy communities). Labor "values" degenerate and there is nothing to replace them. To the extent that class strategy automates management faster and better than production, the moment will arrive when the bourgeoisie will maintain labor in the industrial countries rather than allowing nonwork to emerge! As a result, the spaces of work, nonwork, and leisure begin to intersect in international space in a way that is paradoxically new, and which is only just beginning to assume form and scope.

(i) Thus, the individual is simultaneously "socialized," integrated, subjected to the so-called natural pressures and constraints that dominate him (especially in the spatial context, the city and its extensions), and separated, isolated, disintegrated. A contradiction reflected in anxiety, frustration, and rebellion.

(j) The community assumes two aspects: on the one hand, we have the "public," the "collective," the state, the social; on the other hand, we have the marginal, even aberrant, association of wills. This split can only be resolved through a conception of space; but this solution is still utopian and in no way interferes with the dissolution of those relations that are unable to find their place (their space and their adequate "topos").

This society, unable to transform itself according to the Marxist project, and which will stagnate if it continues in this way unless it chooses (unconsciously) another path, is in the grip of the possible. It is haunted by violence, by the destruction and self-destruction whose principle it carries within itself, and by nonwork, total enjoyment. And last, but not least, by a fully appropriated—that is, *urban*—space.

If, today, we must take up and expand the ideas of the great utopians—Fourier, Marx, Engels—it is not because they revere the impossible, it is because this society bears its utopia within itself, now and forever: the possible-impossible, the possible it makes impossible, ultimate contradictions that generate revolutionary situations that no longer coincide with those predicted by Marx, especially when we consider that they cannot be resolved by the organized (planned) growth of productive forces.

Notes

Foreword

I am grateful to Neil Brenner and Adam David Morton for their comments on an earlier version of this foreword.

1. Henri Lefebvre, *La pensée marxiste et la ville* (Paris: Casterman, 1972).

2. Henri Lefebvre, *Le droit à la ville* (Paris: Anthropos, 1968); translated and edited by Eleonore Kofman and Elizabeth Lebas as "The Right to the City," in *Writings on Cities* (Oxford: Blackwell, 1996), 63–181.

3. Henri Lefebvre, *L'irruption de Nanterre au sommet,* 2d ed. (Paris: Éditions Syllepse, 1998 [1968]; translated by Alfred Ehrenfeld as *The Explosion: Marxism and the French Upheaval* (New York: Modern Reader, 1969); Henri Lefebvre, *La révolution urbaine* (Paris: Gallimard, 1970); translated by Robert Bononno as *The Urban Revolution* (Minneapolis: University of Minnesota Press, 2003); Henri Lefebvre, *Du rural à l'urbain* (Paris: Anthropos, 1970); Henri Lefebvre, *Espace et politique: Le droit à la ville II* (Paris: Anthropos, 1972).

4. Henri Lefebvre, *La survie du capitalisme: La re-production des rapports de production,* 3d ed. (Paris: Anthropos, 2002 [1973]); abridged version translated by Frank Bryant as *The Survival of Capitalism* (London: Allison & Busby, 1976).

5. Henri Lefebvre, *La production de l'espace* (Paris: Anthropos, 1974); translated by Donald Nicholson-Smith as *The Production of Space* (Oxford: Blackwell, 1991); Henri Lefebvre, *De L'État,* 4 vols. (Paris: UGE, 1976–78); Henri Lefebvre, *State, Space, World: Selected Essays,* ed. Neil Brenner and Stuart Elden, trans. Gerald Moore, Neil Brenner, and Stuart Elden (Minneapolis: University of Minnesota Press, 2009).

6. Henri Lefebvre, *Toward an Architecture of Enjoyment,* ed. Łukasz Stanek, trans. Robert Bononno (Minneapolis: University of Minnesota Press, 2013).

7. Lefebvre, *Espace et politique,* 81–97.

8. See Henri Lefebvre, "Perspectives on Rural Sociology" in *Key Writings,* ed. Stuart Elden, Elizabeth Lebas, and Eleonore Kofman (London: Continuum, 2003), 111–20; and Henri Lefebvre, "The Theory of Ground Rent and Rural Sociology," trans. Matthew Dennis, *Antipode* 48:1 (2016): 67–73. For a discussion, see Stuart Elden and Adam David Morton, "Thinking Past Henri Lefebvre: Introducing 'The Theory of Ground Rent and Rural Sociology,'" *Antipode* 48:1 (2016): 57–66.

9. Karl Marx, *Grundrisse: Foundations of the Critique of Political Economy,* trans. Martin Nicolaus (London: Penguin Books, 1973), 479.

10. Manuel Castells, *La question urbaine* (Paris: François Maspéro, 1972); translated by Alan Sheridan as *The Urban Question: A Marxist Approach* (London: Edward Arnold, 1977); David Harvey, *Social Justice and the City* (London: Edward Arnold, 1973).

11. The literature on Lefebvre in English has grown substantially over the past decade. There are discussions of his urban work in the introduction to *Writings on Cities* and in Rob Shields, *Lefebvre, Love and Struggle: Spatial Dialectics* (London: Routledge, 1999); Stuart Elden, *Understanding Henri Lefebvre: Theory and the Possible* (London: Continuum, 2004); Andy Merrifield, *Henri Lefebvre: A Critical Introduction* (London: Routledge, 2006); and Chris Butler, *Henri Lefebvre: Spatial Politics, Everyday Life and the Right to the City* (London: Routledge-Cavendish, 2014). The best account of his work in this area is Łukasz Stanek, *Henri Lefebvre on Space: Architecture, Urban Research, and the Production of Theory* (Minneapolis: University of Minnesota Press, 2011).

12. The writings of some of those already referenced develop Lefebvrean ideas, as does the work of Neil Brenner. See especially *New State Spaces: Urban Governance and the Rescaling of Statehood* (Oxford: Oxford University Press, 2004), and the collection *Implosions/Explosions: Towards a Study of Planetary Urbanization* (Berlin: Jovis, 2014).

1. The Situation of the Working Class in England

1. Friedrich Engels, *The Condition of the Working Class in England*, edited with an introduction and notes by David McLellan (Oxford: Oxford University Press, 2009). [All quotes in this chapter are taken from this edition.—Trans.]

2. Friedrich Engels, *[La Nouvelle] Gazette rhénane*, December 1842, "Les Crises." See also "Esquisse d'une critique de l'économie politique" ("Outlines of a Critique of Political Economy") in *Annales franco-allemandes*, 1844, and "La Situation de l'Angleterre" in the *Annales*, as well as in *Vorwärts*, September–October 1844.

3. [Engels, *The Condition of the Working Class in England*, 15.—Trans.]

4. [Karl Marx and Friedrich Engels, *The German Ideology* (New York: Prometheus Books, 1998), 37.—Trans.]

2. The City and the Division of Labor

1. [Karl Marx and Friedrich Engels, *The Holy Family*, trans. Richard Dixon (Moscow: Foreign Languages Publishing House, 1956), 99. —Trans.]

2. [Karl Marx, "The Economic and Philosophical Manuscripts (1844)," in *Early Writings*, introduction by Lucio Colletti, trans. Rodney Livingstone and Gregor Benton (London: Penguin Books, 1992), 319. Subsequent references are given in the text.—Trans.]

3. [Karl Marx and Friedrich Engels, *The German Ideology* (New York: Prometheus Books, 1998), 37. All subsequent quotations are from this edition.—Trans.]

4. Karl Marx, *The Poverty of Philosophy* (New York: International Publishers, 1992), 89. [All subsequent quotations are from this edition.—Trans.]

5. Karl Marx, *Grundrisse*, trans. Martin Nicolaus (London: Penguin Books, 1973), 692.

6. Ibid.

7. Ibid., 694.

8. Henri Lefebvre, *La Fin de l'Histoire* (Paris: Éditions de Minuit, 1970), 42ff.

3. Critique of Political Economy

1. Especially the *Grundrisse*. However, the Preface and Introduction to *A Contribution to the Critique of Political Economy* (that is, the *Grundrisse*) as well as several other texts relevant to this investigation, were already known.

2. [Karl Marx, *Grundrisse*, trans. Martin Nicolaus (London: Penguin Books, 1973), 85. Subsequent quotes are from this edition. —Trans.]

3. A series of letters by Marx and Engels, from 1853, illustrates just how important this question was to them.

4. Railing against Malthus, Marx shows that colonization in the ancient world corresponds to a surplus population that has nothing in common with what transpires in modern societies (emigration, reserve army of the proletariat, etc.).

5. Today, we may as well admit it, it is necessary to express certain reservations. Weren't the Germanic people, like the founders of Greece and Rome, Indo-Europeans? This is attested by the work of historians and anthropologists, [Georges] Dumézil in particular. However, we cannot deny the tendency of the Mediterranean world (Manichaean) nor certain tripartite features of the society and ideology of Western Europe.

6. [Karl Marx, *A Contribution to the Critique of Political Economy*, trans. N. I. Stone (Chicago: H. Kerr & Co., 1904), 13.—Trans.].

7. Marx, *Grundrisse*, 109.

4. Engels and Utopia

1. [Friedrich Engels, *The Housing Question*, ed. C. P. Dutt (New York: International Publishers, n.d.), 7. Subsequent quotes in this chapter are taken from this edition.—Trans.]

2. [Friedrich Engels, *Herr Eugen Dühring's Revolution in Science* [*Anti-Dühring*], trans. Emile Burns, ed. C. P. Dutt, Marxist Library, vol. 18 (Moscow: Foreign Languages Publishing House, 1962). Subsequent quotes in this chapter are taken from this edition.—Trans.]

3. Engels, *The Housing Question*, 96.

4. Engels, *Anti-Dühring*, 402.

5. Engels, *The Housing Question,* 54.

6. See Anatole Kopp, *Town and Revolution; Soviet Architecture and City Planning, 1917–1935,* trans. Thomas E. Burton (New York: G. Braziller, 1970).

7. Engels, *Anti-Dühring,* 203.

8. [Ibid.; see 231.—Trans.]

5. Capital and Land Ownership

1. [Karl Marx, *Capital,* vol. 1, trans. Ben Fowkes (London: Penguin Classics, 1992), 89–90; emphasis added. Subsequent quotes in this chapter are from this edition.—Trans.]

2. See Henri Lefebvre, *Logique formelle, Logique dialectique,* which exposes in detail the process of reduction and redevelopment (restoration of content).

3. [Marx, *Capital,* vol. 1, 271.—Trans.]

4. [Ibid., 876.—Trans.]

5. See Karl Marx, *Theories of Surplus Value,* vol. 4 of *Capital,* Part II (Moscow: Progress Publishers, 1971), and *Œuvres choisies,* 2 vols., selected by Norbert Guterman and Henri Lefebvre (Paris: Gallimard, 1963–66), 2:213–15.

6. [Karl Marx, *Theories of Surplus Value,* vol. 1, "Addendum 11: Apologist Conception of the Productivity of All Professions" (Moscow: Progress Publishers, 1971).—Trans.]

7. See Marx, *Theories of Surplus Value,* vol . 1, and *Œuvres choisies,* 2:205–6.

8. [Rosa Luxemburg, *The Accumulation of Capital,* trans. Agnes Schwarzschild (London: Routledge Classics, 2003).—Trans.]

9. Which it is for certain doctrinaire followers of Luxemburg and Trotsky.

10. See Samir Amin, *L'Accumulation à l'échelle mondiale* (Paris: Anthropos, 1970).

11. It is obvious that Marx could not have been familiar with modern developments, such as semipublic corporations.

12. [See Karl Marx, *Critique of the Gotha Program* (Moscow: International Publishers, 1972), 10–11.—Trans.]

13. Georges Bataille, *The Accursed Share: An Essay on General Economy,* vol. 1: *Consumption,* trans. Robert Hurley (New York: Zone Books, 1991).

14. [See Karl Marx, *Capital,* vol. 3, Part VI, chapter 46 (New York: International Publishers, [1959]), 544.—Trans.]

15. [Ibid.—Trans.]

16. "In spite of the scope of the disorder, which everyone has felt, provoked by the private appropriation of urban territory, the process of urbanization it implies remains forbidden territory . . . To study the origin of ground rent is to examine urban growth concretely, in a defined situation. . . . The legal status of the soil enables certain individuals, recognized as landowners, to appropriate for themselves the benefits due to urban infrastructure" (Paul Vielle, *Marché des terrains et société urbaine: recherche sur la ville de Tehran* [Paris: Anthropos, 1970], 11–12).

Conclusion

1. Karl Marx, "The Eighteenth Brumaire of Louis Bonaparte," trans. Ben Fowkes, in *Surveys from Exile, Political Writings,* vol. 2, ed. David Fernbach (New York: Random House, 1973), 242.

HENRI LEFEBVRE (1901–1991) was a French Marxist, sociologist, and urban theorist. Many of his books have been translated into English, and several have been published by the University of Minnesota Press, including *The Urban Revolution* (2003), *State, Space, World* (2009), *Dialectical Materialism* (2009), and *Toward an Architecture of Enjoyment* (2014).

ROBERT BONONNO has translated books and articles for more than twenty years. He has taught at New York University and at the Graduate Center of the City University of New York. He is a member of PEN and has received two translation grants from the National Endowment for the Arts.

STUART ELDEN is professor of political theory and geography at the University of Warwick. He is author of *The Birth of Territory* and *Terror and Territory: The Spatial Extent of Sovereignty* (Minnesota, 2009) and editor of Henri Lefebvre's *Metaphilosophy*.